THE CASE OF THE VANISHING BLONDE

Also By Mark Bowden

Doctor Dealer

Bringing the Heat

Black Hawk Down

Killing Pablo

Finders Keepers

Road Work

Guests of the Ayatollah

The Best Game Ever

Worm

The Finish

The Three Battles of Wanat

Hue 1968

The Last Stone

THE CASE OF THE VANISHING BLONDE

AND OTHER TRUE CRIME STORIES

MARK BOWDEN

Grove Press
New York

Published simultaneously in Canada
Printed in the United States of America

First Grove Atlantic hardcover edition: July 2020
First Grove Atlantic paperback edition: July 2021

Library of Congress Cataloging-in-Publication data is available for this title.

ISBN 978-0-8021-5868-0
eISBN 978-0-8021-4632-8

Grove Press
an imprint of Grove Atlantic
154 West 14th Street
New York, NY 10011

Distributed by Publishers Group West

groveatlantic.com

21 22 22 23   10 9 8 7 6 5 4 3 2 1

Contents

Introduction

Newspaper reporting hones an appetite for crime. Good crime stories sell. All the bad things said about them are true—they exploit tragedy, they are voyeuristic, they generally lack any broader social import—but they are unfailingly fascinating.

When I wrote for the *Philadelphia Inquirer*, back in its heyday, when it had reporters based all over the region, nation, and world, we reporters competed vigorously for the paper's limited news hole. You learned fast that a good crime yarn was a shortcut to page one. Our tall, darkly handsome Sunday editor, Ron Patel, would blithely sweep aside the most important news of the week to make room for one. He called them, affectionately, "dirtballs," and would literally rub his hands together with delight as he read them. We dubbed him "The Dark Prince."

Ron reserved a space on the Sunday front page for what he considered the most compelling read in that day's paper, which back then reached well over a million readers. Very often these were crime stories, and this being Philadelphia, there was no shortage of material. There was the one about the kid who was killed when, fleeing a bank robbery in the suburbs on a motorcycle, he crashed when a dye pack in the money bag exploded—he was found mangled and blue; or the dentist who recruited two thugs to cut off half his index finger so he wouldn't be able to work anymore and could collect a big insurance payout; or the transit-bus accident that generated about two times more insurance claims from passengers than it could hold. Ron would strip the headlines of such stories across the very top of page one, over the masthead. The "Dirtball Strip" was coveted real estate for young staffers, and we vied for it weekly, no matter what our assigned beats. I have never lost my appetite for such tales.

"The Incident at Alpha Tau Omega," published in 1983, is from that era; it ran on the cover of the *Inquirer*'s Sunday magazine, an even more coveted spot. At the time, it was a controversial story in the newsroom, given that most men (and newspaper staffs were then, even more than today, predominantly male) thought that any young woman foolish enough to attend a college frat party drunk and tripping on acid could more or less expect to be sexually assaulted. The attitude of some of the editors was, "Why are we making a big deal out of this?" There has been a significant and appropriate social adjustment since then. Incidents like the one at ATO still happen, of course, only now they are often front-page news. Women are still being sexually exploited, but less and less is such male behavior considered somehow normal or understandable. I'm proud of the story, because it got beyond the binary legal argument—rape versus not rape—to grayer and more difficult moral terrain.

Crime has been a part of my work ever since. Three of my books, *Doctor Dealer*, *Finders Keepers*, and *The Last Stone* are of that genre, and several others arguably belong to it—*The Finish* and *Killing Pablo*, about the successful efforts to track down and kill Osama Bin Laden and Pablo Escobar, respectively. Crime has been the subject of many of my shorter works, produced for magazines like the *Atlantic*, *Vanity Fair*, and others.

Over the years I have seen these stories increasingly influenced and often shaped by audio and video recordings. One of the biggest challenges for anyone trying to write nonfiction with the immediacy of fiction is to do it without invention—without expanding on what can be confidently known. In the past, scenes were usually reconstructions, dependent almost entirely on the memory of participants. For a writer like me, audio and video recordings are like gifts from God. When I started as a newspaper reporter in the 1970s, it was rare to have a photo or recording of anything I wrote about. Today it is rare not to have such material. In fact, there is often so much of it that it poses new challenges.

Years ago, recordings or transcripts existed for things like trials, depositions, and hearings, for events closely covered by news organizations, or purely by chance, as with the shaky film footage shot by Abraham Zapruder that captured the assassination of John F. Kennedy and the TV coverage of the killing of his assassin, Lee Harvey Oswald, days later. Such raw material was relatively rare. Today cameras are everywhere. Virtually every store, library, bank, highway intersection or toll booth, stadium, building lobby, parking lot, and city street corner has one or more running continually, and nearly every citizen owns a cell phone capable of recording and publishing, or "posting," videos and still images. Police increasingly wear cameras or have them mounted on their vehicles. The military mounts video cameras on drones that can watch over entire cities, with software that can zero in on specific vehicles or places over time. Increasingly, video exists for the most private of human interactions. Often raw clips of a crime surface before anything else—a sports figure striking a woman in an elevator, a cop shooting a fleeing suspect, a bomb exploding on a busy street—and the footage drives the reporting that follows, much of it increasingly devoted to interpreting and arguing about what the captured scene really shows.

This development has been invaluable for telling true stories. Re-creating past events, crafting fully realized scenes, with characters, action, and dialogue, has traditionally been the hardest part. Unless you witnessed a thing for yourself, the only way to build past scenes was by reconstructing them from written records and the memories of participants. Until fairly recently, this is how all of history has been written down, and the process is, of course, imperfect. Memory is always iffy. Records are sometimes wrong. I learned long ago to seek as many different accounts of a scene as I could before arriving at a version I could trust. My rule, when relying on interviews to re-create scenes, has been to let the reader know, either in the text or in a footnote, where the information comes from—three sources are excellent, two are good, one is sketchy at best. Crafting scenes calls for extreme detail. You can't just ask a source, "What did you do?" Or, "What did you say?" You must ask, "What *exactly* did you do? What *exactly* did you say? What were you thinking? What were you wearing? Was it cold or warm? Night or day? Rainy or sunny? Where were you standing? Why were you standing there? What did the place where you were smell like? Sound like? Which hand did you use?" People look at you funny when you start down this path, but drafting a compelling scene on the page depends on such minute, seemingly irrelevant detail.

Recordings answer many of these questions with certainty. We can now readily imagine a future where any past event can be dialed up and watched in high-definition, with wraparound sound. But even then, we will still need storytellers to edit the raw footage, make sense of it, move beyond what we see and hear. The makers of the 2019 documentary *Apollo 11* relied entirely on the extensive audio and video of the mission recorded at the time, and the filmmakers have said they might eventually place a recording of the entire eight-day mission online for those who want to experience the whole thing as it unfolded in real time. While this would be a very useful resource for historians, I can't imagine anyone else subjecting themselves to it. Most of it will be stupefyingly boring. And even when you have audio or video of an event, you don't know the full story. It takes work to understand even what seems apparent. I once wrote a story about a series of at-bats by the great Phillies slugger Mike Schmidt. I had the opportunity to observe him closely through a succession of games and then to review tapes of his at-bats with him. In my story I described Schmidt stepping out of the batter's box between pitches during one game and taking a deliberate big breath "to calm himself." The fact that he stepped out and took a deep breath was indisputable. I saw him do it, and it was there in a recording of the game. But Schmidt was displeased. He asked me later, "How could you have known why I took a deep breath there? Whether I was anything but calm?" And he was right. I couldn't. I should not have assumed; I should have asked. Even when everything is recorded, writers will still need to do old-fashioned reporting and to exercise the art of storytelling, choosing what to leave in and what to take out, choosing when to slow the narrative and when to speed it up, choosing how to begin and end. An abundance of raw material can make the task both easier and harder.

Two of the stories here are built mostly around such documentation—"why don't u tell me wht ur into" and ". . . A Million Years Ago." The former shows how an aggressive detective, posing online as a mother offering her two young daughters for sex, lures a man desperate for sex to his ruin. The larger question posed by the story is whether J, who indulged online in despicable fantasy, was a criminal or just a troubled soul who posed a danger only to himself. If he was entrapped, as I think he was, the only way to show it would be through the long online dance between him and the detective. Because they left a word-for-word digital trail, it's possible to watch it happen. ". . . A Million Years Ago" is built around a critical interview with Stephanie Lazarus, in which she is confronted with the fact that she was being charged with a twenty-three-year-old murder. Because there was video of the entire session, I was able to construct the story around that dramatic scene.

The others here rely on more traditional reporting methods. The remarkable private detective Ken Brennan, who is featured in three, phoned me cold in 2010. He said he had a great story; was I interested? I receive such calls from time to time. Most are from people who are under the erroneous impression that I (or the magazines I write for) will pay them for material or that I might want to coauthor a story or book with them, which I don't do. When I disabuse them, they retreat. Ken was unfazed. He had a cool story, and he wanted me to tell it. I met with him in Florida, where he laid out for me what became "The Case of the Vanishing Blonde."

It was an amazing story, but I wasn't sure what to do with it. I was writing at the time primarily for the *Atlantic* and *Vanity Fair*. The former tends these days to concern itself with issues of national import, and it hardly seemed like something that would interest *Vanity Fair*, with its fetish for glamour, wealth, and fame. I was chatting with *Vanity Fair*'s editor, the delightful Graydon Carter, when he asked what I was writing. I told him I had a crime story, but I added, "It wouldn't interest you." This turns out to be best line ever conceived for pitching a magazine story. Graydon demanded to see it, and he turned out to have the same appetite for dirtballs as the Dark Prince. "The Vanishing Blonde" became one of the most successful stories I've ever written. It has been translated into other languages and featured in a number of TV adaptations. Ken has become justifiably famous and very sought after. Graydon ran the second of my stories about him, "The Case of the Body in Room 348," and, after retiring from *Vanity Fair* and launching his new online project, *Air Mail*, picked up the third, "Who Killed Euhommie Bond?" Whenever we talk, Graydon asks me for another dirtball.

Like all the stories I write, the ones collected here took me to people and places I would have never seen otherwise. In Lafayette, Louisiana, Susie Fleniken, the widow of the victim in "The Body" story, treated me to her delicious homemade crayfish étouffée; the shamed subject of "why don't u tell me wht ur into" introduced me to a horrid Internet underworld of sexual interplay and predation that I had never heard about; and the

Euhommie Bond story showed how one man's violent death would roil the racially divided small Tennessee city of Jackson. Some of these crime yarns touch on larger social themes—sexual predation, entrapment, racism—but the real reason they exist is that I found them fascinating.

Why I do is anybody's guess. When I was a boy, the local pharmacy stocked the classic magazine *True Detective*, which had garishly illustrated covers (usually depicting scantily clad damsels) and featured work by some of the best crime writers in the country. My parents wouldn't let me read it. So they are probably to blame.

December 2019

The Incident at Alpha Tau Omega

The Philadelphia Inquirer,
September 1983

I t was February 18, a sunny Friday afternoon. The brothers
of Alpha Tau Omega had partied straight through to the
purple dawn. It had been ATO's first successful "pub night" of
the semester. A few of the boys were idling in a first-floor bedroom, downing the foamy dregs of a near-dead keg.

Even the house seemed hung over. Crud from hundreds of
dancing feet caked the floor. Discarded gray cups of unquaffed
beer wafted an odor stale and unpleasant, like the taste of a dry
mouth the morning after a few too many. The ATO house is a
muscular mansion of burgundy stone, ornate but a bit down-at-
the-heels, that commands a key corner lot at Thirty-Ninth Street
and Locust Walk, right at the residential heart of the University
of Pennsylvania campus. Drape a few sheet banners between
windows above, roll a dented keg or two onto the porch, and you
have it. The house was home to one of Penn's most bumptious
communities of "Greeks."

Social graces they had not. But fun, they had plenty. Among Penn's twenty-seven fraternities, ATO was known for its rowdy, lowlife crew. Taking only enough pledges to fill the rooms of their beloved house, ATOs recruited quietly on a back-pocket jock network. Most of them were varsity athletes. The thirty-one members of ATO saw themselves as the tightest group of brothers on campus. They studied together, played together, partied together, and, now and then, got in trouble together.

It was one week after the big snow. Andrea Ploscowe, a good friend of the ATOs, had come over to hang out. It was always fun talking to Andrea.

And today there was much to talk about. Last night's party had, in a way, stepped over the edge. There was this girl, this strange girl named Laurel, and . . . well, in the vernacular, there had been a "train." Nobody was sure at that point how many brothers had had sex with the girl. Five? Six? Maybe ten. Word whispered around all that morning. Some brothers were disturbed, others delighted—it was the kind of event that enhanced house lore. Still, others weren't sure what to think. Andrea hadn't heard. When she mentioned that she had seen this girl Laurel dancing pretty wildly early on at the party and that Laurel had seemed so strange, the brothers just started telling her about it.

Right away Andrea's response shocked them. She was horrified. She wanted details. She wanted to know exactly what had happened.

The brothers asked her why, and what she said next stung— a sudden slap in the face from a friend. It was the first hint of the ordeal they would all face in the months ahead, an ordeal that would be, for many, the most difficult experience of their young lives.

Andrea had answered, abruptly, "For my own information, I'd like to know who the potential *rapists* in this house are."

Andrea Ploscowe's outrage was the first splash on a still pond. Ripples of angry accusation would ring out across campus to city newspapers and television stations and from there across the nation. "Gang rape at Penn" was hot news nationwide. Almost overnight, this group of college boys had become the object of such intense, widespread disdain that they scarcely believed that the callow faces they saw in the mirror were their own. Lumping the ATO brothers in with the perpetrators of a notorious New Bedford, Massachusetts, barroom rape, a columnist for *Time* magazine wrote, "All subhumans are created equal."

Forget "alleged." The word "rape" echoed with salient horror from a place like Penn. It is Ivy League, one of the country's oldest and most prestigious universities. Its nearly ten thousand undergraduates are the cream of America's secondary schools.

These were college boys. If the charge was untrue, what was at the bottom of it? Were the ATO brothers criminals or merely callous? Were they sacrificial lambs to some new and unrealistic definition of rape, framed by feminist harpies? And if the charge was true, were they guilty of an overtly criminal act, or of acting out a common male fantasy, licensed and approved by the bawdy reminiscences of their fathers and uncles and older brothers, broadcast by subscription TV stations into their living room and glorified in the glossy color photos of popular skin magazines—a fantasy that, this one night, became real and left everyone feeling sick and wounded and more than a little wrong?

Rape. Once that word is out, the accusation hurled, it becomes important to know, first, what really did happen that night at ATO, and, second, why.

Laurel Brooks has an aura of sadness that envelops those closest to her. She is so clever and funny, yet can at moments be so utterly certain of life's ultimate emptiness that a conversation with her is vertiginous.

Different doctors give different names to her underlying malaise, but one trait stands out: Laurel is far more likely than most people to do something on impulse.

She is pretty. Delicate. Green eyes, fair hair worn curly, down to her shoulders. Given the tenor of her talk, Laurel's very wholesomeness unsettles. A high school cheerleader. Varsity letter. Played in the school band. Class officer. Among the top ten in her graduating class. *Big deal.* She holds these credentials in contempt. *Here I am, Laurel Brooks. Twenty-two. Senior, University of Pennsylvania. Big deal.*

Drugs were fun. Booze was fun. Dope was fun. Looking back on it, Laurel figures she spent most of her time in school high. *High* school, get it? Loads of laughs. Laurel led a kind of double life. She came from a successful family of professionals. There was all this healthy pressure to succeed, and Laurel worked hard to succeed. She *had* to do well.

But there was a part of her that was her alone and that asked, urgently, "Why?"

Will Gleason met Laurel at a party in January, but he didn't really fall in love with her until a few weeks later.

An accomplished student, Will bears his scholarship lightly. Daily workouts keep his slight frame taut. At times he feels like he has been borne along through his twenty-one years by tides he cannot fathom. Inner tides or outer tides? Usually when he acted he did not know why. His ambivalence bugs him, but at his age, confusion is often honest and even charming, and he knows this too. His hair is blond, and his eyes are blue, and his smile is quick and frequent.

The party that January night was for "punks," pop nihilists in drag. Will was looking for a girl. Laurel was at the party, walking around looking weird. She was wearing her "tripping garb," a baggy black crewneck sweater bummed off her roommate and black-rimmed black sunglasses to shade her acid-primed pupils. Will had a buzz cut, blond locks cropped to the scalp. He was rolling a cigarette when Laurel walked up and asked, by way of introduction, "Are you Australian?"

Will had grown up in a New York suburb not twenty miles from Laurel's hometown.

"No, I'm not Australian."

"Are you European?"

Her questions were making Will laugh.

"Well, I lived in Europe for a year."

She walked away. Just a screwball, Will figured, but when she came back and asked him to dance, he said OK. Laurel spent the night with him.

"She liked me," Will said. "I could see that. Laurel was a wreck the night before, but when she looked up at me that morning—I'll never forget the look she gave me in the morning. She gave me a look that just melted me, I'm tellin' ya. She looked at me like there was all the horror and desperation in the world behind those eyes. And she just kept staring at me, and she said things to me like how beautiful I was, and I thought, 'Well, this is the psychedelia here, telling me how beautiful I am.'"

They saw each other often over the next two weeks. Will thought she was witty and pretty and fun. But he was alarmed at her drug use and drinking.

"She bought a ton of acid off of some guy, and she just had hits of acid laying around her room. She would just wake up in the morning, I guess, and feel like she just didn't want to face the day and just chew hits of acid. I don't know. That's what she was into at the time."

It alarmed him more the more he cared. On the phone one night when she called, drunk, he yelled at her, "I ain't got time for this! I ain't got time for these crazy people and getting drunk!" But the truth was that Will was beginning to warm up to her, despite his misgivings. It was a strong undertow, drawing him in, down.

One day, he considered taking the acid from her.

"I thought it was going to kill her. She tripped within two weeks about ten times. Then I thought, 'It's not my right to take the acid away from her.'"

That was the day of the ATO party. Will's father was in town, staying at the Holiday Inn near the university, so Will planned to have dinner with him and hang out at the hotel. He talked to Laurel on the phone that afternoon. She said she was going to a frat party with some friends. Strange, Will thought. He didn't think Laurel was the type to go to a frat party.

"What are you doing after the party?" he asked. "I want to see you."

"OK," Laurel said.

"So, what time do you think you'll be done with the party?"
He remembers she told him about midnight or one, or later.

"Call me as soon as the party is over, and I'll come get you
wherever you are, and we'll go home, go to my place."

Laurel said OK. Will had dinner with his father that night.
In the hotel room they watched *Hill Street Blues*. But Will was
restless. During the commercials he phoned Laurel, hoping to
catch her. She had left. He thought about looking for her at the
party, but he didn't like frat parties.

So Will said goodbye to his dad when the show was over and
went home. Before he went to sleep, he took the phone from the
table in the hall and set it on the floor inside his bedroom door.
He wanted to make sure it would wake him when she called.

Music on the party tape was old rock and new wave. Dance
music. A racing beat like the sound of a speeding heart was
backdrop to events of the night.

Henry Groh was helping set up the stereo system downstairs when Laurel showed up. It was ten thirty.

"She was wearing dark glasses and this big black sweater
and jeans with patches all over them. She seemed like one of
these new wave–type chicks, you know, like, on South Street,
you see these people walking around? She looked like one of
these type people."

Gradually the first floor filled. Dancers jostled drinkers.
People talked in shouts. It was fun. There were beer kegs in the
basement and trash cans lined with plastic and filled with purple
punch spiked with grain alcohol.

Andrea Ploscowe had come with a friend. Before they left for
another party, Andrea remembered spotting a girl in dark glasses

and sweater dancing oddly from room to room, drawing attention to herself. It looked to her like the girl was on something. But there was nothing unusual about somebody drugged out at a party.

In the wildness later, when the song "Suffragette City" came on, it was the signal for the brothers to do their circle dance. The idea was to join arms in a big circle and go round and round, faster and faster, chanting "Ho! Ho! Ho!" or singing along, dizzy, with David Bowie, round and round until one brother broke for the middle and all would follow, leaping that way and this, limbs akimbo, asses over elbows into a great comical heap. Most of the partygoers had seen this act before. It was an ATO staple. So when the circle formed, all others backed off. Evidently Laurel didn't know, because she ended up stuck in the center, bewildered. Big Maury Rath, in the crush, grabbed Laurel hard on her upper arm and flung her aside when the heaping began.

Early on, a group of partygoers had some laughs with Laurel by spinning her around in a dark room and refusing to let her out. When she threatened to scream, they pointed her through a doorway that led only to an interior bathroom. She screamed. In her state, with acid and alcohol in her brain, treatment like this was scary and profoundly disorienting. But then she found her way out, and all seemed OK again. She also remembered falling down a flight of stairs.

Through the night the party roared. It eased and quieted slowly until, by after four, most of the crowd had gone. Small groups clustered in upstairs bedrooms afterward to share personal stashes of dope or grain alcohol or whatever. Already, it had been a good night.

*   *   *

Versions of what happened next differ significantly. After Laurel cried rape, most of the ATO brothers, on advice from their lawyers, had little to say. Laurel has never publicly talked about what happened. Her version of the incident in this article is drawn entirely from interviews with university officials and students in whom she confided. They say the brothers carried Laurel upstairs when she asked for a place to sleep. She had sex with one of them willingly. Then, one by one, a group of men had sex with her. Laurel pleaded throughout to be left alone.

Without denying the basic facts of what happened, the brothers contest this coloring of them. In their version, reconstructed by six of them several months later, Laurel stayed in the house long after all but its residents and their closest friends had gone. The party was over, but she was still in a partying mood.

They have thought and talked much about what happened next. Lou Duncan came out of a bathroom that adjoins his bedroom and saw Laurel, her jeans off, sitting on the lap of his roommate, Ed Roush, who was asleep in a chair. Duncan said Laurel was kissing Roush, trying to awaken him. Duncan approached her and pulled her away. Then Kip Moran came in. Moran is a wiry young man of serious manner. He has a natural flair for leadership. The brothers respected him and trusted his judgment. Moran helped get Laurel dressed again. She told him she wanted to lie down and sleep, so he offered her the couch in his room upstairs. He showed the way, helping her navigate the stairway.

There is an icebox upstairs near Moran's room where beer and grain punch were stashed. Henry Groh walked up to check the fridge and then went looking for Moran. His bedroom was dark, but by the red pilot bulb on the stereo, he could faintly see Moran in the room with Laurel, whom he recognized from the party earlier. She was fully dressed and sitting on the couch. Moran was crouched over the stereo.

"Yo, Kip! What's happenin'?" he asked. Groh reconstructed what happened next.

"I started going into the room, and we just started talkin'. She said, 'What's your name?' I said, 'Bags.' That's my nickname. And, um, then we just talked about stupid stuff. I was, I had been drinking, and, I wasn't drunk, but I certainly was at least affected, you know. I wouldn't have driven in the condition I was in, but I can still remember what happened."

Moran left the room as Groh talked with Laurel.

"When I went in there, there's no doubt that, like, I would have been open for, like, a sexual contact kind of thing," Groh says. "And this girl started to, I don't know, come on to me, in some sense. It wasn't the kind of thing where all of a sudden you start ripping each other's clothes off or anything like that. Like, just the normal way of sexual proceedings, you know, occurred. But she was, she was really receptive. She was getting real excited, having a good time, you know . . ."

By most accounts, Groh was the first to have sex with Laurel that morning. Laurel's roommate later said that Laurel had confirmed that she had had sex willingly with one man that morning, although she didn't remember who he was.

The brothers say that Moran came back upstairs at that point and that Groh left the room. Moran then had sex with Laurel.

Although the ATO brothers deny that word spread about the girl upstairs, a file of young men—about eight or nine— showed up either to watch or to have sex with Laurel during the next several hours.

Maury Rath said he came up, like Groh, to check the icebox for leftover grain punch. He too found Moran and Laurel talking in the room. As he entered, Moran again left.

"You could see just by the light of the stereo, so the room was illuminated a little bit. There was someone there, who happened to be Laurel, half sitting on the floor, half leaning on the couch, you know, just kind of reclining there. I walked in, and I thought, 'Why is this person here?' I didn't know what was going on. I am just assessing the situation. As I came in, she said to me, 'Who's there? Who's that?' And she goes, 'What's your name?' And I said, 'Maury.' And I approached her. As I came closer to her, she reached out to touch my arm. It seemed like she was making advances at me—she was, like, in a rumpled state of dress at that point too. I thought, 'What the hell is going on here?' And then I finally, as I moved closer to her, I realized the girl was obviously coming on to me. Not often does a girl come on to you like that. And that situation was, like, really odd, and my first reaction was, 'What the hell kind of girl would do this?' and, you know, 'Who knows what she's been doing or what's going on?' And I just shied away from the situation. I just said, 'Sorry,' and I just walked out."

Rath says he then walked to his room, drank some punch and went to bed. He had to leave early the next morning to catch a bus home and see his girlfriend.

Interviewed together, the brothers give similar accounts. One by one, they happen upstairs alone and enter the room, where Laurel makes "advances." One by one, they either have sex with her or they don't. Jake Daubert claims he was unable to get an erection. "Though I would have to admit that I had sexual contact with her, I could not complete the act, and I did not have sex with her. I basically was embarrassed. It was the first time I had to face impotence, all right? And I was terribly embarrassed about that."

Interviewed separately, the brothers offer conflicting details in their stories. For instance, several say they encountered Laurel alone in the room, while others describe being present for those encounters. But despite important inconsistencies, a rough picture emerges. For most of the time, more than one of the men were present. Most of the brothers involved were aware that this was not a simple sexual encounter. All insist that they considered Laurel's behavior to be strange—and even, in Rath's case, disgusting—but they judged her to be sober and alert and willing. They say Laurel left the room at one point, wrapped in Moran's robe, and walked to the bathroom. Then she came back. They say at one point Laurel did ask them to stop. She said she wanted a cigarette. Daubert gave her one. She smoked it, chatting with them, and then the sexual activity resumed. One of the brothers made sure that there were condoms available on a table in the room for the others. Venereal disease was something they all feared. For one brother, Nick Allen, it was the first time he had had sex with anyone.

"It didn't seem that odd to me," Allen says. "Because of the stories I've heard from other fraternities and from guys in the house and from the movies you see on TV. We have this Select TV in the house, and there's soft porn on every night. All the guys watch it and talk about it and stuff, and it didn't seem that odd, because it's something that you see and hear about all the time. I've heard stories from other fraternities about group sex and trains and stuff like that. It was just like, you know, 'So this is what I've heard about, this is what it's like, what I've heard about.' That's what it seemed like, you know."

Daubert, who had seen Allen with Laurel, says he felt "really weird and bothered," because Allen, theretofore a virgin, had been able to have intercourse with Laurel while he had not. Months later, he was still troubled.

Daubert is not the only brother who felt pressured to perform. A number of those present struggle to describe an odd "mood" during the incident. As the sexual acts occurred, others stood by outwardly oblivious, as if pretending that nothing unusual was happening. Standing by, one by one, they saw but did not watch.

"When I walked into that room that night, I knew what was going on," says Al Mitchell, one of those involved. "Not through anybody telling me, but there was a different kind of excitement going on there, a different mood. And Laurel is there in a bathrobe. She obviously has no clothes on under there. I knew what was going on. I'm not stupid. It was more of a crazy mood. It wasn't normal. It wasn't blatant, though. It was weird. I knew what was going on without ever having been told. I think everyone knew. I was kind of in a spell. But what I have to stress here is that it never, in any way, resembled the way in which you have some guy having sex with this girl, coming off and saying, 'OK, you're next.'"

They use different words, but the feeling is the same. It was as if their responses were foreordained. They were acting out some brute ritual they can neither understand nor explain. It had something to do with belonging to the fraternity and, deeper than that, with what "fraternity" meant, what it meant to belong. Feminist writers argue that implicit in any exclusive organization of men, especially in a society dominated by men, is an assumption of sexual supremacy—an assumption that armies, clubs, and fraternities have been acting out in gang bangs for centuries.

In their most polished version, the brothers depict themselves more as victims of a series of seductions than assailants in a train of rapes. If Laurel's version is true, most of them are simply lying. Laurel's friends and school officials who spoke with her later said she repeatedly protested and asked the brothers to stop. One of the brothers involved tried to be helpful about the disparity: "The guys are very wary of what could happen to them. They are very distrustful. You don't know what they have been through. I am under the impression that the truth is somewhere in the middle. Cut it in half. I don't know if what you come up with will be exactly what happened, but it's the fairest thing to do."

What almost certainly happened that night at the ATO house was that a troubled young woman came to the party tripping on acid. She got even higher drinking. Despite the brothers' later accounts, it must have been evident to everyone who saw her that she was not acting in a normal, sober way. There are two things one can to do with a person in this state: either help her or take advantage of her. What happened appears to follow the classic pattern described in sociological studies of gang rape— absent any overt display of violence. The leader of the group asserted control and set the pattern for what followed. The men proceeded to act out the standard scenario, having sex with her one by one, observing each other in the act, relying upon peer pressure to overcome any moral repugnance. They felt obliged to do so. Several of those involved who did not have intercourse with Laurel nevertheless allowed their brothers to assume they had, right up until the university brought charges against them, and it became, no matter how injurious to their egos, important to confess. It is probable that Laurel, in her condition, protested weakly. She may have even actively participated.

Although the absence of violence in the ATO incident makes it substantially different from traditional rape scenarios, the definitions of rape are changing—socially and legally. A woman no longer has to show cuts and bruises and broken bones to be considered a victim. It is now sufficient that she is intoxicated enough so that she cannot consent and that the man knows it. The very idea of six or seven men having sex with one woman begs explanation more from the men than the woman— especially when she later alleges rape.

At about six thirty a.m., Moran walked Laurel downstairs and showed her out the door. She was upset about losing her sunglasses. She could not see well without them. Daubert remembered watching from an upstairs window as she walked off toward her dormitory. Then he lay down at last to sleep.

The sun was up. Inside the ATO house there were mostly good feelings.

"At that point it was, like, we had had a real good party, if you know what I mean," Groh says, "the first good one that semester."

Joan Vila, one of Laurel's two roommates, saw her later that morning.

"Laurel looked horrible. Her face was really bloated, really *really* bloated, like after having cried hours and hours, when your tear ducts have been operating for so long and all the fluids are in your face and the blood rushing around and everything looks all mottled and terrible."

Joan said, "Are you OK? You look terrible."

"Really?" Laurel seemed shocked.

When Laurel gave Joan the black sweater she had borrowed the night before, they both noticed a gaping hole under one arm. Laurel apologized and offered to buy Joan a new one. She said she had fallen down during the party and torn it. Joan wondered how a person could tear the armpit of a sweater falling down, but she didn't ask. No sense making Laurel feel worse.

Laurel came back to the ATO house that afternoon to search for her missing sunglasses. She prized them. They resembled a fashionable and expensive brand.

The brothers were shocked when she came in. They weren't sure how to act or what to say. Al Mitchell helped look for the glasses and remembered being bothered by Laurel's apparent indifference to what had happened. He gave her a beer and asked how she felt. He said she answered, "Fine." Very casual.

"No, I mean, how are you feeling deep down inside?"

He recalls that Laurel answered slowly, saying, "I want to feel like I'm embarrassed, but I can't right now." And then she talked about the four hits of LSD she had taken before the party and how she had a headache now and felt ill.

Andrea walked in then. She didn't know yet what had happened. She had just stopped by to schmooze with the guys that morning. She didn't know Laurel, but she remembered her from the party. Andrea recalls how bad Laurel looked that day. Her eyes were red and her skin was puffy. Andrea joked to Laurel that she had seemed really *into* the party the night before, and then added, knowingly, one girl to another, "Oh boy, I can remember times when I've been drunk and I've lost things and I've woken up with bruises and I didn't remember where the hell I got them from." Laurel showed Andrea some bruises and scrapes she had picked up the night before. Andrea remembered in particular a vicious bruise on the inner part of Laurel's upper arm. As she and Laurel and Al talked, a few of the other brothers gathered. Even though she thought Laurel was a little weird, Andrea was trying to be nice. It was clear from Laurel's conversation, which Andrea and the brothers found so strange, that this girl lived on the outer edge of even their permissive social world.

Andrea was worried about her. She encouraged Laurel to stop by the Penn Women's Center to see Carol Tracy, the head of the office, who counseled women at the university. Laurel then left, after jotting down her name and phone number in case her glasses turned up.

It was not until after Laurel left that Andrea learned of the sexual episode. She was saying how troubled the girl seemed, and Roush said, "She got boned last night."

"Several times," Daubert added.

They called what happened "group sex." Andrea was revolted. Their attitude—*these were her friends!*—galled her. She didn't want to believe it had happened. She asked for details.

The brothers asked her why she wanted to know, and her response was the first time they heard the accusation. They recoiled angrily when Andrea said the word "rapists." *Rape?*

"Hold on just a minute, Andrea," Mitchell said, anger and surprise steeling his voice. "Don't go jumping to conclusions and calling things rape when you don't know the facts." His sharp tone rebuffed Andrea, and she backed off.

Andrea was used to playing House Feminist for ATO. The title was half joking and half not. Andrea had these two natures—she calls them her "Jekyll" side and her "Hyde" side.

On the one hand, as a nineteen-year-old sophomore, she was just coming into her own as a feminist. Andrea was articulate and intelligent and ambitious. That was what she called her Jekyll side. Andrea was also a looker, something that had not escaped the boys in ATO. She was shapely and pretty, with pale green eyes and dark blonde hair. If she liked a guy enough, she would sleep with him. She had gotten involved with three different ATO brothers over the past year. That was her Hyde side.

Jekyll Andrea was often outraged by the macho posturing of her friends at ATO, but Hyde Andrea was flattered by their eager attentions. She enjoyed challenging them. Here was this chick who had the potential, on any given night, of putting out, but who demanded to be treated as an equal. Andrea made their double standards uncomfortably obvious. Whereas if one of the brothers got it on with three different women in one semester he might be a hero, a woman who got it on with three different ATO brothers was supposed to steal off quietly into the night. They had gotten something off her, right? But Andrea wasn't even shaken. She was thinking about moving into the house that summer. Who was getting what off whom?

Andrea was drawn up in this double game. She knew the guys had two ways of seeing women. Steady girlfriends were respected. Other women, the kind the brothers were always trying to make, were called "hos," a sort of chuckling little word of obvious derivation that doubled as an ATO cheer when they did the house circle dance or scored a goal in intramural sports. Girlfriends and hos. Andrea, who was then nobody's girlfriend, wanted it clear that she was nobody's "ho" either.

So, over the next few days, Andrea kept asking questions. And the more Andrea heard, the more her gut response seemed right.

There was something grotesque and unnerving in the arrogance of these guys. No. Something was wrong. Andrea wasn't sure yet what the word for it was, but the more she heard, the more she thought the right word for what happened might be "rape."

She had been keeping an account of the incident from the first day she learned of it, writing it all down, disgustedly, in her diary. Now she wrote,

> They vehemently insisted it wasn't rape, that no one forced her, & and that she in fact told them that that was what she wanted. She was saying, "F— me! F— me!" I can't believe that! Besides, she was so screwed up she probably couldn't have said her own name. If they had sex w/ her they were really taking advantage. I can't believe that any woman could want that. It's beyond me how she could ask for something like that. Maybe she was too screwed up to care, but it seems more likely that she was too screwed up to know what was happening to her at all & if that's the case it's not group sex, but rape.

A voice in the back of her head whispered, "Talk to Laurel. Talk to Laurel."

Will Gleason awoke Friday morning wondering why Laurel hadn't called. All night the phone had sat silently inside his bedroom door. She had said she would call him. He was miffed.

He finally called her at five p.m. She apologized and told Will she wanted to go to a dance that night. When he stopped by her room to meet her, he was surprised to find her still in bed.

"I walked in and kissed her on the cheek. She was very out of it. I remember saying to her, 'You smell like sour milk.'

"She said, 'Thanks a lot.'

"'What happened? Are you still hung over? I mean, what happened?'

"She goes, 'I got beat up at the party last night.'

"I said, 'Beat up!'

"She told me she was tripping, and I thought about when I met her, and I thought about how big those guys are, and then she said, 'I got beat up. Pushed around. They ripped my sweater.'"

"It didn't cross my mind that she could have possibly been raped. I say, 'How did it happen?'

"And she said, 'They locked me in the room and wouldn't let me out. And they kept pushing me around, and I kept telling them, 'Leave me alone! Leave me alone!'

"And I said, 'Oh, great.'"

At that point Will didn't want to hear any more. If there had been an ugly scene, he didn't want to know about it.

They went to the dance but left early. Laurel complained she was too sore to dance. The next evening, Saturday, they went to another party, tripping on mushrooms. Will had never taken a drug like that. It unleashed powerful sensations. Great gusts of energy whirled in him, and he felt a passion for Laurel that was overwhelming. He was still high when early that morning in bed she told him.

"She says to me, 'What happened at ATO the other night, I was raped.' It's like four in the morning or five in the morning, and she says it to me. 'I've been raped.' I flipped. I mean, this is the girl I just decided I loved, regardless. I mean, it was the first night I was able to go, 'Ahh, I love you! I love you! I love you!'

and grab her and say, 'I love you! I love you! I love you!' And
it totally wiped me out. I mean, I got up out of bed, and I was
walking from room to room, and I couldn't touch her, and I was
revolted, and it was really awful.

"'How many guys?'

"She goes, 'I don't know.'

"'*You don't know!* You were raped? Well, call the police! We'll
call the police now!'

"She goes, 'No, no.' And she's trying to make light of it—this
was the reaction she had, you know, put it out of her mind. She
said, '*GIRL GETS ABUSED*—these things happen.'

"I'm going like, 'Take this seriously! This is awful! This is
horrible! Take this seriously! I want you to be grieving like I
am! I don't have to grieve all your pain for you! This is what you
should be feeling!' And I was, like, in anguish . . ."

On Tuesday morning, Andrea spotted Laurel sitting with her
roommate, Joan Vila, in the Hardee's in Houston Hall, hunched
over a crossword puzzle. She sat down at the table with them and
broached the topic by saying, "I spoke to the guys after you left."

Andrea remembered Laurel seemed surprised. She asked
what the brothers were saying.

"Don't worry about that, but how are you?"

"Not great."

"Do you feel you were taken advantage of?"

"Yes, of course. I was raped."

Joan was furious. She told Laurel that she had known something was wrong that morning when she saw her. The three
young women huddled. Laurel's version wasn't like the brothers'

story at all. She had only vague recollections of the night, but from what she remembered and Andrea knew, the women were able to piece together the incident and identify the players. Laurel complained that her glasses had been taken early on, so in addition to being out of it on the acid and beer, she couldn't see well. She talked about how a group had trapped her in a dark room and spun her roughly. Laurel said that she had been carried upstairs, and that she remembered the brother who did that. She didn't know how many of the brothers had had sex with her, but she remembered what some of them looked like.

Andrea didn't know how much to tell Laurel. The girl seemed so sad and isolated. She told her not to worry about being pregnant, because the guys said they all used rubbers.

Laurel was distressed that the brothers had been talking about the incident, and in such detail! She wanted to know what else they were saying. Andrea told about the in-house ragging and the rumors of a "train." Laurel was furious. Joan said Laurel could not let them get away with it, and urged her to press charges. Joan was hot. Andrea tried to calm things down.

"Look, you've got to get yourself some attention. You've got to get yourself to a doctor. You need medical and psychiatric attention immediately. Don't even think about pressing charges right now. That's not important. What's important is that you get yourself some help."

Laurel was still reluctant. She didn't want to get anyone in trouble.

"Don't worry about them," Andrea said. "You have to worry about you right now."

She urged Laurel to see Carol Tracy at the Penn Women's Center. Her office was in the same building upstairs. As soon as the women parted, Laurel mounted the steps and made an appointment to see Tracy.

That night Andrea wrote in her diary, "How can Laurel understand as I do that the guys had no idea of the kind of damage they did w/out realizing it. They are so ignorant in my eyes, so malicious in hers. Like Bags said, 'We were drunk. What do you expect us to do? Carry her home?' They have no idea how much hurt they can do despite their lack of bad intentions."

The Penn Women's Center, founded ten years ago after a gang rape on campus, is an unusual agency. Carol Tracy and the three women on her staff are part of the university administration, but they are designated "advocates," charged with bringing a feminist perspective to campus issues. Tracy, a soft-spoken but hard-minded woman in her thirties who became head of the center six years ago, is in her last year of law school at Temple University. A fair woman with brown hair, Tracy eschews makeup and welcomes controversy—it makes people think.

She had already been tipped off about the "train." A student had told her that there was talk going around the men's locker rooms. It sickened her, but experience had taught her not to expect much. A young woman in that position would be unlikely to come forward. The pressures were just too much.

So Tracy was surprised when Laurel appeared that afternoon. Her heart went out to the student. She seemed utterly broken, so nervous and fragile. Her voice cracked with emotion, and her hands trembled—clearly, a young woman in deep trouble. Tracy could sense how Laurel had wrestled with the ordeal, first pretending it didn't happen, then sliding out of shock into less anger than pain. It sounded to Tracy like rape. Mindful of procedures for reporting a crime, she phoned Ruth Wells, a campus police officer, and asked her to come over. It was late when Wells arrived, near dark. As Laurel recounted the tale, she began to stutter. First a little, then more.

Throughout, Laurel told Tracy, she kept asking them to leave her alone, to get off her, to stop. She displayed the bruise on her arm and showed where the backs of her arms were raw from rubbing the rug.

Tracy didn't want details. She tried to calm Laurel, assuring her that she would get help. Wells told Laurel that the next step was a police report. Laurel said she didn't want to prosecute. Tracy didn't want Laurel pressured, so she quickly interjected that she understood Laurel's reluctance to go that route. It would be terribly difficult. Still, both women told the girl that the incident must be reported, even if it went no further.

"It was a felony, and we were obliged to report it," Tracy said. "Laurel would have to go to the hospital." Wells phoned Bill Heiman, head of rape prosecution for the district attorney's office. Laurel repeated her story to Heiman. Tracy remembered Laurel insisting that she did not want to prosecute. Before he hung up, Heiman told Tracy he would not take action unless he heard from them again. Before she left, Laurel agreed to let the rape unit at Thomas Jefferson University Hospital examine her the next day. There, as part of normal procedure, she would tell her story to police.

But when Laurel left, Tracy suspected that if anything would be done about this incident, it would have to be done on campus. Laurel had dropped the matter squarely in Penn's lap.

*   *   *

On Wednesday, Laurel went to Jefferson Hospital to be examined and interviewed. The University of Pennsylvania began its investigation.

Laurel had told Carol Tracy about Andrea, and Tracy sent word to Andrea that she wanted to see her. Andrea came over right away. She explained her mixed emotions to Tracy. The older woman listened sympathetically and then told Andrea firmly that, no matter how she felt about the fraternity, she would have to tell whatever she knew to Ann Hart, the campus judicial inquiry officer, whose job is to investigate misbehavior by students and recommend punishment.

So Andrea talked to Hart, who seemed disgusted. In a way, it was a relief for Andrea to find a mature response that seemed to validate her own anger. When she had tried to explain her anger to the brothers, they told her that she was acting like a silly child. At last Andrea began to feel that her first reaction was appropriate.

If there was any question in Andrea's mind about where she stood in all this, whether she was trying to stay friends with the ATO brothers and accept their version of what happened or whether she was conspiring to have them punished, indecision vanished that afternoon when she stopped by the house. Posted on the second-floor landing were minutes of the last weekend's house meeting.

Brothers had recorded "highlights" of the previous week's exploits, sexual and otherwise, full of allusions to the incident.

"Things are looking up for the ATO sisters program," the first item read. "A prospective leader for the group [whom

Andrea deduced meant Laurel] spent some time interviewing several Taus this past Thursday and Friday. Possible names for the little sisters include 'The ATO Little Wenches' and 'The ATO Express.'"

It turned Andrea's stomach. Another of the items referred to one of the brothers involved, a Catholic, noting that he "started Lent on the right foot by making sure he had fish on Friday." Posted with the highlights was a recent letter from the Fraternity/Sorority Advisory Board, which regulates the affairs of these groups, regarding the forthcoming service awards. On it someone had written, "We serviced Laurel."

Andrea was infuriated. The glib crudity confirmed her worst instincts about what the guys had really thought. She had heard the stories circulating in the men's locker rooms. She had heard of the sign placed above the lockers of two ATO members that read "39th Street Station," a reference to the location of the ATO house and the "train." She had wanted to believe that her friends were above all this, but after seeing the "highlights" she knew which side she was on. That clinched it. There was no turning back.

Andrea plucked the "highlights" paper and the letter off the wall and stuffed them into her pocket. She was trembling. On her way out, she ran into a few brothers, so she sat down on the outside steps with them, afraid she would somehow appear conspicuous by just striding past. When one of her friends walked by, Andrea shouted across to her, asking if she was going to a women's conference meeting the next day. One of the brothers turned and grabbed Andrea playfully and gave her a gentle push down the steps.

"Hey, none of that women's stuff," he said.

Andrea took advantage of the shove to leave the steps. She turned and, with what she knew he would interpret as play anger, answered haughtily, "We're discussing violence against women!"

She walked directly over to Houston Hall, photocopied the papers, and took them to Ann Hart. In her diary that night she wrote, "Ann seemed pleased w/ me, disgusted w/ the guys." And after Hart had repeated what she knew to the campus police officer Ruth Wells, and after Andrea had shown Wells the "highlights" paper and the letter, "the consensus was in, these guys are sick," Andrea wrote. "I felt a little embarrassed. I mean I've been partying w/ them all year & they're my good friends. I guess I've lost my perspective of what constitutes normal behavior. I know rape is wrong. But I've had some good times there. Sometimes partying 'til you drop seems to be the thing to do . . . this is unreal."

The trouble broke out at ATO house the next day. Until now the brothers had enjoyed quiet notoriety from the incident. The one or two who felt bad had kept their remorse to themselves. Andrea's carping was just a bother, just what they had expected from their House Feminist.

But that afternoon the slap of Andrea's initial accusation was multiplied a hundredfold. One of the brothers described the scene:

"We were sitting around about four o'clock, you know, late afternoon, just sitting around talking, and Moran comes in looking like he's been shot through the heart or something like that. He's got some paper in his hand, and he says, 'We're in trouble, we're in such big trouble. You guys won't believe it. Boy, this is really bad.'

"And we said, 'Well, what is it?'"

"And he shows us the charges, you know, these charges against us."

Moran had been summoned out of class and served with two letters from the administration. One tersely informed him that a complaint had been made to the university against him and eight other ATO members. Their names were listed on the bottom. It instructed him to be in Ann Hart's office that very hour with a copy of the minutes of the last ATO meeting—the one that produced the infamous "highlights," which, unbeknownst to Moran, Andrea Ploscowe had already turned over. The letter said appointments with Hart the next day should be arranged for the other brothers named. The second letter, from Alan Thomas, the acting director of fraternity and sorority affairs, asked him and the same list of brothers to contact the campus security office immediately to arrange interviews with the Philadelphia Police Department. *The Philadelphia Police Department?*

Moran was astonished and frightened. He could deduce what the complaint was about, but it was confusing. A few brothers listed had not been involved in the incident. One had been out of town when it happened. He wondered what kind of story had been given to the administration. Without knowing what he was charged with, he wasn't sure what he should say. It was frightening. He stopped at a phone booth to phone a friend on the law school faculty. His friend advised him to say nothing until he conferred with a lawyer. But Moran's first impulse was to tell the truth. He believed that he and others couldn't get in trouble once the school knew what had really happened. So he went to see Hart.

He no sooner started talking to her, though, than he felt he had made a big mistake. Right off he admitted some things that could prove damaging. He acknowledged he had had sex with Laurel that night, and others in the house had too. And he got the impression that this was all Hart really wanted to know.

Hart had butted heads with ATO before over milder complaints. The brothers didn't like dealing with her. The year before, a fraternity member allegedly involved in a fight had taken Hart and the university to court over disciplinary action she had taken against him. He won the case. Most of the brothers figured that Hart, if not the whole university, had it in for them. Maybe they should get lawyers. But lawyers cost money.

Panic spread through the house that evening. Moran had the brothers named in the complaint signing up for half-hour sessions with Hart the next day. Despite his misgivings about Hart, he argued that once the truth was known, they would not be in any trouble. After all, the charge—*rape?*—was ridiculous, right? A few of the more skeptical brothers weren't buying it. They were busily trying to contact lawyers. They were convinced, the more they thought about it, that Hart would try to make them sacrificial victims to a feminist crusade against fraternities.

Then Maury Rath had an idea. One of the faculty members they had phoned for advice had suggested that if they didn't trust Ann Hart, they should go over her head. Why not go straight to the top? The matter was certainly serious enough. The more they talked about it, the more the brothers agreed. So a delegation was chosen to see the university president, Sheldon Hackney. Right away.

* * *

Hackney had been at Penn for just over two years. In keeping with his goal of making the sprawling university more of a cohesive academic community, Hackney was the first Penn president in the twentieth century to live on campus.

Five ATO brothers walked through the cold night to Hackney's renovated mansion and rang the bell at about ten p.m. A student waiter, dressed in a tuxedo, answered the door and told the brothers the president had dinner guests. The brothers said they had to see Dr. Hackney right away.

The student disappeared inside for a moment, then returned to say that Hackney would see them later that night.

The phone rang about a half hour later, and the group trudged back over to meet with the president. Hackney is a dark, handsome man, tall and slender. If his position and impeccable appearance were intimidating to the brothers, his gracious Southern manner put them quickly at ease.

They came in, a group of about five or six. Hackney said later, "They were quite somber, sober, so I knew something was worryin' them. And they described their version—they did not go through everything—but they described some version of the incident."

The group told Hackney that a number of brothers had had sex with Laurel the night of the party. They characterized Laurel as the aggressor and said her charges were absurd.

Hackney listened, disturbed. He had not heard of the incident.

"They said that they came to me for advice because they had been contacted by the judicial inquiry officer and asked to come in and talk about this. And they did not know much about the system, the judicial system, and were really unsure about whether they should trust it or not. They simply wanted my advice. I told them that they ought to go and talk to the judicial inquiry officer and tell the truth, and they would come out all right."

Hackney meant, of course, that if they cooperated with the procedures, they would be treated fairly. None of the group was happy with this advice. They expressed their worries about Ann Hart and about how, with Carol Tracy's involvement, this whole investigation had the look of a feminist lynching to them. The process seemed to be moving too fast, at any rate, and they were uncomfortable with it. They didn't really understand what was going on. Hackney told them that if they wanted some assurance about the system or some information about how it worked, they could talk to George Koval, Ann Hart's boss, the acting vice provost for university life. He said he would help arrange a meeting.

Hackney said later that this offer amounted to nothing. The students could have asked for a meeting with Koval on their own and would have gotten it.

But the brothers were delighted. They knew that Koval was Hart's boss. They felt that the president had intervened on their behalf. Hackney's offer to call the vice provost and arrange a meeting had, as far as they were concerned, pulled a string that placed Hart's investigation on hold, indefinitely. Koval would listen to reason.

None of them kept their appointments with Hart the next morning. Over the weekend they got their stories together and hired a lawyer.

The story broke in the *Daily Pennsylvanian*, Penn's student newspaper, on March 7. An administrator had leaked the news

over lunch to editor Peter Canellos just a few days after Laurel
reported it.

Canellos had the story nailed down within a week. One
of the people he asked about it was Carol Tracy, but she wasn't
helpful. The break came when an ATO brother, evidently under
the impression that the newspaper knew more than it actually
did, agreed to tell what he knew if his name was not used. After
that, Canellos called Tracy. The Women's Center director had
talked to Laurel after Canellos first came snooping by.

"I told her that I would not give out any information, but
that the story was likely to break anyway," Tracy said. "I asked
her if she wanted me to speak in her defense, when and if it did.
She said yes."

So Tracy listened to the ATO version that Canellos's reporters had gathered. She found it very predictable. It was, of course,
all Laurel's fault. She had been willing. She had been the aggressor. If she had been gang-raped, why would she have come back
the next day? Why did she wait four days to report it? Tracy
explained how rape victims usually begin by trying to pretend
that nothing had happened. Laurel's reaction had been typical.

What they didn't seem to understand was that even if Laurel
had seemed willing—and Tracy found that hard to believe—it
could still be rape. Tracy had thought about little else for the
last two weeks. More than she wanted to see anyone at ATO
punished for what happened, she wanted them to understand
this: It was rape because of the state Laurel was in. It was rape
because she was unable to consent. Tracy had studied the stat-
ute, and it was pretty clear about that. She didn't feel sorry for
the ATO brothers at all. She didn't believe that men's sexual
passions could get so aroused by a woman in that condition that

they couldn't control themselves. She saw the brothers' story as a standard male myth, a rationalization of behavior. This was a girl who had taken acid and drunk all night and who was looking for a place to lie down. The guy who took her upstairs had first helped to dress her. *She couldn't even dress herself!* And then he and the others proceeded to have sex with her. The kind of frenzy or whatever that's associated with group sex is something that Tracy couldn't begin to identify with. The right thing to do should have been simple enough. They should have taken Laurel home. Instead, they had taken advantage of her, ruthlessly. Tracy had talked to enough people who were there that night and who saw the state Laurel was in. But there was this standard problem with rape, one that almost ensured that anyone but the most overtly violent rapist would go unpunished. Rape is not treated in graduated degrees the way murder is. Tracy knew enough about what happened at the ATO house that night to realize that this was not the kind of rape that was intentional or premeditated, the kind that was easily prosecuted in court. It was not like five men attacking a woman on the street, dragging her into an alley, and raping her at knifepoint. No, the law didn't allow for gradations with rape, but this was rape just the same.

So Tracy sounded off. The story led the campus paper that morning with a big headline: "Student Charges Gang Rape / U. investigate incident at ATO party." Tracy had gotten the last word.

Tracy said the fraternity should be removed from campus and called the alleged incident "the single most awful event ever reported to me in 15 years at Penn. It was uncivilized, inhuman, reprehensible behavior that should shock the conscience of the university community . . ."

* * *

Two friends who saw Laurel that day described her as being "numb" and "in shock." The newspaper had called her the night before to tell her that the story was being published the next day and that she would not be named. But nothing could have prepared her for the big headline and the furor that followed.

Her father showed up that afternoon and took her home.

In the two and a half weeks between the day the *Daily Pennsylvanian* story broke and the day ATO got a formal hearing before the Fraternity/Sorority Advisory Board, the brothers became notorious nationwide.

The incident provoked an instant, virulent response that stunned the fraternity members. As they learned more about Laurel, about her drinking problem and her drug problem, most of the brothers felt bad about what had happened. A few, discussing it among themselves, decided that they had not done the right thing that night. But none of the brothers believed that the incident could be even remotely considered rape. If they had taken advantage of Laurel, and in retrospect it seemed that they had, they had not done so knowingly. Far outweighing any feelings of remorse, however, were feelings of bitterness and anger—toward the feminists, the press, and the university officials who they believed were persecuting them. Still, they had been advised to keep their mouths shut. They just had to take it.

Three days after the story broke, students organized a rally to protest violence against women. More than five hundred people crowded into Houston Hall to register disgust. Among them was a group of ATO brothers who considered themselves as anti-rape as anyone. They winced when the first speakers denounced their fraternity and called for them to be thrown off campus. They felt like guests of honor at a slow lynching.

As for the facts, each of the brothers had taken a lawyer along for the interviews they had rescheduled with Ann Hart. One by one, they repeated the same denial: "I did not have *forced* sexual contact with the young woman."

Hart's findings were presented late in the afternoon on Wednesday, March 23, before the Fraternity/Sorority Advisory Board, which is composed of faculty, alumni, and fraternity and sorority members. The board would decide whether any infraction of the university's rules had occurred. The hearing continued in a warm room well into the night. Photographers and reporters waited in the hallway outside.

The university's complaint against ATO was based on the agreement under which Penn recognizes chapters of national fraternities. Under this agreement, fraternities are obligated to "accept collective responsibility for the activities of individual members" if misbehavior by those members "is knowingly tolerated by the members of the fraternity and is in violation of the University's Code of Conduct."

"By the end, we had heard, basically, two separate stories," one of the board members recalled. "In the version prepared by Ann Hart, the young woman was drugged and drunk and clearly out of control. She was taken advantage of in that state by a number of fraternity members. In the ATO version, the young woman appeared to be in full control of herself and initiated sexual activity with a number of brothers over a two-and-a-half-hour period that morning. The fraternity characterized it basically as a series of separate sexual encounters that took place voluntarily."

There were two questions before the board. Did the fraternity members do what they were accused of doing? And if they did, did they act responsibly?

"My feeling was, I was upset because I didn't have all the information," the board member said. "I didn't feel like I knew enough to make a reasonable decision, because each of the two stories was so different."

Nevertheless, the board voted to recommend that ATO be suspended until January 1984, which meant that it wouldn't be allowed to recruit new members, or "rush," until then or to hold parties or benefit dances. The board also recommended that all officers of the fraternity and any members directly involved in the incident be thrown out of ATO, and that direction of the fraternity be turned over to ATO alumni. That penalty, the board members felt, was severe enough. Later, the ATO brothers said that penalty would have been mild. They would have been delighted with it.

Koval, however, went further. On Friday, March 25, he withdrew recognition of ATO, the most serious penalty the university can impose on errant fraternities. The national organization could not reapply for recognition until September 1984. And even if recognition were granted then, all current members were barred from joining any future ATO chapter at Penn. Further, the brothers were all ordered to move out of the house by the end of the semester. For all practical purposes, ATO was dead.

A special panel appointed by Hackney the following Monday investigated the charges that the university had brought against individual members of the house for violating the school's code of conduct. There was never a hearing. Everyone involved was aware that hearings on the charges—the brothers had the option of requesting open hearings—could prove exceedingly embarrassing to everyone involved: to Laurel, the brothers, and the school. The incident had already exacted a toll on everyone.

So there was a settlement. The specifics of individual agreements are private, but some of the general terms are as follows: The brothers involved never admitted guilt. In return for the university's promise not to take further action against them, the brothers agreed to perform community service, to complete a reading list of material pertinent to the issues raised by the incident, and to participate in group discussions of those issues. Some of the brothers who would have otherwise graduated in June will not receive their diplomas until they satisfy these commitments.

"It wasn't trivial," said a person familiar with the settlement. "The requirements will take time to fulfill. Individuals who couldn't arrange to stay around after graduation will be able to meet the requirements where they've gone, but they still have to do the work. The general idea, I guess, was that the best thing would be for the fraternity brothers to take something positive away from the whole experience."

When Carol Tracy heard of the settlement, she was so angry that she felt like resigning. Some of those involved in the case had been angry all along over what they saw as Hackney's intervention in the matter. As terms became generally known, they reinforced a notion on campus that the university was reluctant to take the matter seriously. Hackney defended the decision to keep details of the settlement secret. Without knowing more about what actually happened, the community could not fairly assess the appropriateness of the penalties, he said. Months later, the issue still troubled him. In Hackney's two years at Penn, the ATO incident was the first that kept him awake nights.

Laurel Brooks did not return to classes on a regular basis that semester. After the investigation, she spent some time in a psychiatric hospital, where she became convinced that she was an alcoholic, and when she checked out she stopped drinking for nearly two months. Then, one day in May, after an argument with her parents, she abruptly left home and returned to Philadelphia.

Within several days, Laurel began drinking again. Before the week was out, she was back in a hospital for psychiatric treatment. She had retained her own lawyer and was exploring possible grounds for taking civil action against the university and the brothers involved in the incident.

Weeks after Laurel checked into the hospital, Will Gleason was still wrestling with his emotions. He felt uneasy in some way he couldn't quite define. He felt, somehow, as though he was just as much to blame for what happened to Laurel as any of the fraternity brothers.

"I've thought about this a lot," he said. "What difference was there between what I did and what happened to Laurel? Laurel was drunk and tripping the night I met her too. I was out looking to pick somebody up, for some sex, you know? I mean, Laurel was, of course, willing when she came home with me. I don't know. But where was the difference when she woke up in the morning with me, who she liked, and she looked at me and I was 'beautiful' and

I was nice to her, and that other morning she woke up alone in horror. I don't know. The line's fine. I'll never . . ."

He didn't know how to finish.

At the end of May, the ATO brothers who had planned to stay in Philadelphia over summer vacation moved out. A few months later, they won an injunction against Penn that allowed them to return until the issue is resolved in court. The brothers, however, remained pessimistic about ever living in the stone mansion again.

Andrea Ploscowe was working as a waitress in a small restaurant off campus during the summer. The incident, and what was known on campus of her involvement, had made Andrea something of a feminist heroine. She felt certain that she had done the right thing, but still, Andrea was troubled. There was a stubborn remorse in her for betraying her friends at ATO. She missed them and was disappointed that, after everything, they seemed to understand so little.

"I don't think they've learned a damn thing," she says.

The brothers were bitter, certain of their own innocence and convinced that the university was spineless, more concerned with avoiding bad publicity than in seeing justice done. They felt a mixture of sorrow and anger for Laurel. Most reserved the better part of blame for Andrea. They were convinced that it was she who had talked Laurel into considering the incident rape. Andrea had it in for them. They were sure.

Yet, despite their bluster, it was clear that the brothers were affected in ways they are still reluctant to admit. One hopes someday to be a doctor. After a long and spirited defense of his own actions and those of his friends, he was asked what a good doctor would have done, faced with the scene he witnessed that morning. He spoke slowly, looking down at the table.

"A good doctor would have acted to stop it," he said.

Perhaps, as more time passes, as they work through their feminist reading lists and participate in their assigned group discussions, they will work through the impact of what happened that night. For the brothers of Alpha Tau Omega, things may not work out so badly. Laurel Brooks is still under psychiatric care. For her, it is still too soon to know.

When this story ran in 1983, I changed the name of the victim and all of the fraternity brothers, and also of Andrea Ploscowe, at her request. Andrea died of cancer in 2017. She became a lawyer and remained an activist for feminist causes throughout her life. I decided to use her real name for this new publication of the story. I have had no contact with Laurel or any of the fraternity brothers since, and often wondered what they think about this episode years later. Carol Tracy is the longtime executive director of the Women's Law Project in Philadelphia.

"why don't u tell me wht ur into"

Vanity Fair, December 2009

Detective Michele Deery works in a cubicle in the basement of the Delaware County courthouse, in Media, Pennsylvania. The only window is high on the wall, over a tall filing cabinet, and opens into a well below ground level. The space feels like a cave, which has always struck Deery as about right, because her job is to talk dirty online to strange men.

Deery seems altogether too wholesome for the work. She has athletic good looks, with tawny skin, big brown eyes, and long straight brown hair that falls over her shoulders. Her parents sent her to Catholic schools, and her mother, a retired district judge, now jokes that she wants her money back. Her daughter's beat is in the vilest corners of cyberspace, in chat rooms indicating "fetish" or various subgenres of flagrant peccancy. One of the many false identities Deery has assumed online is something truly rare, even in this polluted pond—that of a middle-aged mother of two prepubescent girls who is offering them up for sex. Baiting her hook with this forbidden fruit, she would cast the line and wait to see who bit.

It usually didn't take long. Despite the improbability of the scenario, men would begin vying for her attention the minute she logged on, night or day. Deery would begin a dialogue, dangling the illicit possibility, gauging how serious her mark was. There were "players," those who were just horny and despicable, and there were "doers," or at least potential doers, the true bad guys. The goal was to identify the latter, hook them, and then reel them in, turning them into "travelers." A mark became a "traveler" by taking the all-important step out of fantasy and into the real world, at which point his behavior moved from merely immoral to overtly criminal. When the mark delivered himself for the promised real-world rendezvous, instead of meeting a mother and her young daughters, he would find a team of well-armed, cheerfully disgusted Delaware County police officers. As a fantasy, her come-on was overbaked—not one daughter, but two! It is doubtful that such a woman exists anywhere, and yet men fell for it. Her unit had a near 100 percent conviction rate. It was rare for those she caught to even challenge the charges in court. The bulletin board over her desk displayed mug shots of her catches, very ordinary-looking men, facing the camera wide-eyed with shock, staring out at the fresh ruin of their lives.

Which leads to the case presented here. One of the stunned faces in that array belongs to a man I will call J, who would spend a year in prison after Deery plucked him from the precincts of sin—in the case presented here. Both Deery and J were willing to speak about it openly and at length; transcripts of online chats and police interrogations were also made available to me. This account reflects what they and others said about themselves and their actions. It is two stories really, very different yet unalterably joined.

Shortly before six o'clock on the evening of Monday, September 19, 2005, Deery went to work in her cave, logging in to Yahoo and expertly navigating its public chat rooms. In one of the many rooms labeled "fetish," she logged in with the suggestive screen name "heatherscutiepies." At this time of day, the weirdos were coming home from work, bellying up to their home computers.

She received three instant messages in quick succession from someone using the name "parafling":

—*hello*
—*may I ask what your into or looking for*
—*NOTHIG is taboo to me*

Parafling had the detective's interest. Fluent in the shorthand of instant messaging, she answered:

—*well why don't u tell me wht ur into*

Entrapment has long been a factor in the enforcement of vice laws, which seek to punish behavior that is furtive and widespread. Such ordinances answer society's quest for moral clarity, positing a direct parallel between two sometimes unparallel things: right versus wrong, and legal versus criminal. There are many morally reprehensible things that are not criminal. It's never hard to find sinners. There are many, many more of them than there are criminals. Evil fantasies can become crimes only when acted upon.

Taking that step from thought to action is key, and many police stings are about presenting sinners with the opportunity to act. American courts have long recognized the right of police to invent ruses, especially when society feels threatened. Sting operations flourish in a climate of fear. Courts and lawmakers become less scrupulous about legal niceties and even basic fairness. The more frightening and reprehensible the threat, the more license and latitude are given to the police.

For a variety of reasons, few of them valid, the child molester has become the preeminent domestic villain of our time. Deery's work is part of a national effort. In 1998, in response to growing fears of sexual predation online, Congress provided funding for the Department of Justice to create the Internet Crimes Against Children (ICAC) task force, which among other things provides federal grants to local police departments for programs to find and apprehend online predators. In practice that means looking for people who potentially fit the mold—people who seem as if they might be poised to molest a child even if they have not yet done so. This leads unavoidably into the gray area of thoughts, intentions, and predispositions—and into the equally murky realm of enticement and entrapment. It is a way of conducting police business that, without extreme care, can itself become a form of abuse—in which the pursuer and the pursued grow entangled in a transaction that takes on a gruesome life of its own. This is the terrain explored by Philip K. Dick in his classic short story "The Minority Report," and in the Steven Spielberg movie based on it, in which an official government department of "Precrime" identifies, charges, and jails people on the basis of anticipated actions.

As Jad, one of the policemen in the movie version, says, "We're more like clergy than cops."

* * *

Bingo! A woman!

That was J's reaction when the tag "heatherscutiepies" popped up in a window at the top of his screen.

He had peeked into a number of active chats to see how many women were there, and logged in to the ones with a promising ratio. His screen name, parafling, was a nod to paraflying, the use of the tiny parachute/tricycle flying machines he had once or twice flown. It was the only really different, exciting thing about him. He imagined it was like a colorful lure on the surface of a pond.

He was excited to see on-screen that this woman, calling herself heatherscutiepies, lived in his state, Pennsylvania, and was thirty-nine years old. He had immediately tapped her with three messages, and she had responded:

—well why don't u tell me wht ur into

The sun blazed in from the window to his back porch. J had about an hour before his wife would be home from work. She knew nothing of his cybersex life, or if she did, she ignored it. A burly, round-faced man of forty-two, with a thickly muscled neck and shoulders, thinning hair, and a goatee, he was seated before the computer in their living room in a small, two-story town house in suburban Philadelphia. J had just finished a long day of repairing copy machines, driving from one job to the next. This hour at home was his time, a quiet interlude before his wife came in the door from her job at the local hospital. He would then have to deal with her until about eight o'clock, which is when she usually retired upstairs, leaving him alone again with his computer and his obsessions.

J didn't sleep much. The steroids he was injecting to help him bulk up made his heart race and filled him with explosive energy and lust. He felt like a walking hard-on. The Internet was his only outlet, and it had become a compulsion. He would open up three or four windows into sexually oriented chat rooms, looking for a woman to talk dirty to him. If he got lucky in one of these early-evening sessions, he would arrange to continue with her later that night after his wife went upstairs. Then they would play together, cooking up an erotic stew. He would enjoy an extended period of arousal and then masturbate. This was his routine. This was his sex life.

In the years he had been dipping into these chat rooms, J had learned a few things about the women who entered them. They were outnumbered, and they were skittish. J was convinced that everyone, down deep, had twisted sexual desires, and he had reasons in his own life for believing this: his first sexual relationship, as a teenager, which had lasted five years, was with a slightly older girl who liked sadomasochistic play. In this sense, women were no different from men, except they were more reluctant to show themselves. The ones who entered the fetish rooms had desires that were very specific. As J saw it, men were eager and up for whatever, but women were picky. They were looking to scratch a particular itch. He knew that if he answered the query from heatherscutiepies wrongly, she would simply stop responding. Her question was polite nibbling. His response was critical. He had chatted about this precise situation online with other men, comparing notes on opening moves, and the safest approach seemed to be simply to announce that you were into "everything," right off the bat.

He typed:

—I am into bondage s/m breeding incest young rape spanking you name it

Nine seconds later came her response.

—cool.

Hooked! Then she asked another question:

—where in pa?
—west of philly, you
—oh no kiddin im in philly burbs.. just moved outside city not 2 long ago.

This carried a jolt of erotic possibility. Ordinarily, J had no idea where the person he chatted with was—this was part of the chatroom's appeal. Many participants had no desire to be identified or found. Yet proximity, for J, spiced the game with a chance at something real. His chats had led only once before to a real encounter, three years earlier. Acting out the online scenario for real had felt awkward. He had done as she asked, and they had had sex, but he left knowing he would never do it again. Reality was stark and messy—it had texture and odor and harsh lighting. Acting out fantasy roles for real felt phony and wrong. It lacked the purity of the idea. The episode had taught him to stay on his side of the line.

That was before he had started injecting steroids, however. Now the sheer weight of lust was straining him to his limits. One of his coworkers, a former marine, had counseled him that women were drawn to thickly muscled men, so he had thrown himself headlong into bodybuilding—pumping iron, ingesting growth supplements, and ignoring even the modest dosage restraints urged by experienced gym rats. The results were striking and obvious: his neck, shoulders, and arms were bursting out of his shirts. He found himself picking fights with strangers, screaming at drivers who annoyed him on the road. But his transformation had had none of the desired effect on women whatsoever. It had only redoubled his lust. The news that this willing woman was nearby—a real woman!—came with the exquisite thrill, all but forgotten, of potential.

Heatherscutiepies wrote him another message. Both used the slapdash vernacular of Internet chat, with its shorthand spelling, frequent abbreviation, and minimal punctuation, which often led to confusion. She explained why she had left Philadelphia for the suburbs.

—*wage tax was kickin my ass*

Then she added, sardonically, the online acronym for amusement:

—*lol* [laugh out loud]

J wrote:

—*damn so very close.*

She asked:

—*ever try any of ur taboo's or just fantasy?*
—*yes I have had sex with cousin and about 10 years ago
i did breed a married woman because hubby did not want
too, so I did,lol nd never heard from hr after that*

None of this was true. He had learned from earlier chats that if he said he had never tried a thing the woman would stop responding. It was best to claim to have done everything. Besides, making these things up came easily to him. In the years he had been chatting sexually online, J had learned to ease fluidly into a realm of complete make-believe. Already he had covered two of the categories of taboo he had listed at the outset, incest and "breeding"—having sex with a woman to get her pregnant. Neither had seemed to click. All he knew was her screen name, that she lived nearby, and that she was thirty-nine. If he was going to line up some serious sex talk with her later, he would need to quickly find what enticed her. Even in this shameless arena there was courtship. So he asked for some sexual direction, and then followed immediately with two more ordinary conversation queries, showing a willingness to talk about anything she wished.

—*what are you into,,,,,,,,,,,,are you married,,,,kids???*

She responded:

—*no kiddin*

This was meant as a humorous lament, but J took it as a question. He thought she was asking whether he really wanted to know.

—*yep no kiddng.*
—*im divorced 2 girls*
—*WOW age??*
—*im 39*
—*no sorry girls,lol*
—*8 11*

J wrote three lines in rapid succession:

—*I saw your age*
—*yummmmmmmmmmm*
—*tell me what do you look like??*

He followed this immediately with a request for a picture, and she responded:

—*if I get 2 know u a little bettr ill send*
—*are you looking for a man to be daddy and take you and the girls???*
—*no just 4 sum fun*
—*ok can you just describe yourself then to me, and I respect that too*
—*dont want any permanent feature here*
—*cool*

J was zeroing in. She had two little girls and her screen name was heatherscutiepies. The "cutiepies" were apparently her girls. He had instantly made the connection; she was turned on by the idea of a man having sex with her children. If this was her turn-on, he was neither shocked nor repulsed. Years of immersion in chat rooms had inured him to strangeness. Words were J's game. Perverse ideas. He had never been aroused by images. He was not a porn addict. What gripped him was a woman limning her darkest dreams—for him.

This was the essence of his personal fetish, a woman baring all—not the private parts of her body but the private parts of her mind, her unique sexuality, her heart's most peculiar desire. It drove him wild. He was after heatherscutiepies' itch, her singular taboo. The key to her erotic zone, the thing J sought to provide

in return, was complete acceptance. His chatting partner had
to feel free to go anywhere with him. That was now his goal.
To get her there without turning her off or scaring her away. To
that end, he would become whatever heatherscutiepies wished.
The idea was to turn her on. Then he could work gently toward
some of the things that pleased *him*.

He typed two messages:

—*would you like to be like side lovers doing you and the
girls??*
—*maybe breeding you and the oldest or anything like
that?*

That clicked. There was no mistaking it. He received four
responses from heatherscutiepies in quick succession:

—*yea*
—*no breedin as of now*
—*good god*
—*im strapped for money as it is*

Down in her cave, Deery decided that she had a live one. When
they were finished chatting, she would type a request on the
courthouse's internal network for a warrant to obtain his IP
(Internet Protocol) address. Then she could get private information from his Internet provider.

He had mentioned "young" right off the bat. That was important. The rules against entrapment forbade her from suggesting
the criminal act, but he had brought it up himself. Then he had
asked about the "girls," her imaginary children. When she gave
him their ages, he had replied, "yummmmmmmmmm."

Except, on closer examination, the import of that expression of appetite was less clear. Sometimes as two people typed out a conversation, with the slight delay that entailed, dialogue overlapped. When she told him she had two girls, he had initially asked, "WOW age??" She had immediately responded, "im 39," thinking he was asking about her. That line was typed at 5:57:07. Eight seconds later he corrected her, "no sorry girls,lol" and then typed two more messages in the next eleven seconds, "I saw your age," and "yummmmmmmmmm." Between those responses, at 5:57:20, she had typed, "8 11." His comment "I saw your age" came one second after she had given the ages of her girls, so they had been typing those lines at virtually the same time, and J's "yummmmmmmmmm" had come just five seconds later. Was he reacting to her, or to the ages of her girls? On the screen, and eventually on the printout, the sequence made it look as if he was reacting to the ages of the girls, when in fact it was hard to tell.

It became more clear thirteen seconds later, when he asked what she looked like and for her picture. His focus seemed to be primarily on her. But then, when he asked if she wanted him to "take" her, he had included the girls. Was he asking if she wanted him to have sex with her and the girls, or was he asking if she was looking for a sugar daddy, someone to *take care* of her and the girls? The abbreviated, highly colloquial syntax left plenty of room for interpretation. The detective played it safe and assumed he had meant the latter. But then, right away, on his own, he had mentioned, "doing you and the girls." That was evidence. Parafling was soliciting sex with two minors.

* * *

J next sent her a description of himself, including the size of his penis—"7." ("Why did they all exaggerate?" Deery wondered. It was so lame.) He pushed for more information—asking for her "measurements."

Deery typed that she did not know them.

To J that seemed odd, but then, in this Internet space, who wasn't? She kept deflecting his interest in her. Was she just being coy, or was she really more into the idea of his having sex with her girls? He wrote:

—*LOL so tell me if and when we meet when and how you would like this*

Again, she did not spell out exactly what she craved, so J continued to make conversation. He asked her about her two jobs—she had told him she cut hair at home and worked as a bartender at night—and then tried to reassure her that he was honest, candid, and serious. He explained his screen name and then urged her to make clear whether she was serious about wanting to meet with him in the real world:

—*if you want cyber then say so, want real say so*

What stuck in his head were those four quick responses when he had suggested becoming "side lovers." It wasn't so much what she said, but the responses signaled eagerness. And she lived close by. He began to entertain for the first time in years the possibility of meeting a real woman and having real sex. His typing grew more rapid and error-prone.

—*I am looking for exaclty what you are offering, no strings noperment be there when ever you want I will please you and the girs*

She wrote:

—u ever playd w yung?

This woman wanted him to talk about having sex with little girls. It could not be clearer that it was a package deal. She came with her "cutiepies" or not at all.

The first entrapment defense upheld by the US Supreme Court was in 1932, during Prohibition, when the defendant, a paper-mill worker named Randall Sorrells, was convicted of selling whiskey during a social encounter at his home in Clyde, North Carolina. Sorrells had received several longtime friends, who brought along a visitor from nearby Charlotte. The men were World War I veterans, and the newcomer, who was actually a Prohibition agent, had served in France in the same infantry division. Convivial conversation ensued, and at one point the agent asked his host if he could get him some whiskey. Sorrells told him that he "did not fool with whisky." The agent was persistent. Again he was rebuffed. After more talk, the agent appealed to Sorrells's old comradeship and again pleaded for help in getting a drink. Out of fellowship, Sorrells relented. He left the house and returned with a jug. When he handed it over and took the agent's five dollars, he was arrested.

Convicted at trial, Sorrells appealed, finally winning his case in the country's highest court. Writing for the other justices, Chief Justice Charles Evans Hughes called the methods used in his case a "prostitution of the criminal law." He noted that the crime for which Sorrells was prosecuted by the government was "the product of the creative activity of its own officials."

Since that ruling, the issue of entrapment has come before the Supreme Court several times, and arguments have traditionally turned on what has become known as the "subjective" and the "objective" tests. The subjective test for entrapment considered primarily the defendant's state of mind: Was the subject inclined to commit the crime anyway? The objective test centered more on the action of the investigators: Were their methods sufficient to induce an otherwise law-abiding citizen to commit a crime? If a defendant had a history to suggest he was predisposed to committing a crime, it was very hard to show that police efforts alone were responsible. Both rules left much room for interpretation, and neither was likely to help someone accused of a particularly repellent crime.

The most recent Supreme Court ruling on entrapment, in 1992, went a way toward knocking down the subjective test. In 1987, a Nebraska man named Keith Jacobson ordered a magazine called *Boys Who Love Boys*, which was described as a publication containing pictures of "11- and 14-year-old boys engaged in sexual activity." The magazine didn't exist: it was the invention of the US Postal Service. Federal agents arrested Jacobson after he went to the post office to pick up his order.

Jacobson had come to the attention of federal agents because, years earlier, he had ordered a magazine called *Bare Boys*. At the time such photographs were not illegal. But a record of the transaction had been enough for agents to target Jacobson with come-ons for the imaginary magazine. He had taken the bait only after repeated attempts by two separate federal agencies. The issue of entrapment was raised at his trial, but Jacobson was convicted in federal court of receiving by mail sexually explicit material depicting minors (by then illegal), even though the magazine he had ordered didn't exist. His earlier purchase weighed heavily against him, because it suggested a predisposition toward such material—the subjective test. There was no evidence that Jacobson had ever approached a child sexually.

His conviction was overturned by the Supreme Court, in a decision that struck a lasting blow to the subjective test. In the majority opinion, Justice Byron White wrote: "In their zeal to enforce the law . . . Government agents may not originate a criminal design, implant in an innocent person's mind the disposition to commit a criminal act, and then induce commission of the crime so that the Government may prosecute." The justices did not address either the subjective or objective tests directly, but they made it clear that predisposition alone did not mean guilt, particularly if the crime was suggested by police to begin with.

Regulation of sting operations tighten when the crime concerned is less menacing. Judges and jurors are inclined to sympathize with a defendant tempted by ordinary vice. It's not coincidental that the very notion of entrapment, putting brakes on law enforcement, emerged from a case involving alcohol at a time when the American public was increasingly fed up with Prohibition. When a more sordid offense is involved, or one of greater social concern, the police can get away with more.

During the past fifteen years, as the Internet has made inroads into every facet of modern life, the fear of online child predation has grown far out of proportion to the actual problem. The belief that sexual deviants by the tens of thousands are prowling the Internet in search of children to entice and corrupt, and that their ranks are increasing rapidly, has won broad popular acceptance. The most widely cited statistic is "one in five," as the number of children who have supposedly been approached by a sexual predator on the Internet. The origin of this figure is the Department of Justice's National Center for Missing and Exploited Children, which first reported it in 2001. Five years later the center amended the result to one in seven, but by either measure the figure suggests nothing less than an epidemic.

Until you look closer. The actual question posed in the department's Youth Internet Safety Survey asked teenagers under seventeen whether they had received an "unwanted sexual solicitation," which was defined as follows: "a request to engage in sexual activities or sexual talk or give personal sexual information that was unwanted or, whether wanted or not, made by an adult." Since "adult" in this case was defined as anyone seventeen or older, the definition included many would-be high school Romeos, predators of a highly conventional and not particularly dangerous sort, and also took in a strain of intimate gossip familiar to all teenage girls. As the study's authors themselves noted, half the solicitations came from other teenagers. Not a single solicitation led to actual sexual contact. Violent sexual predators hunting children are out there, as they have always been, yet they remain blessedly rare, and most young people flee such strangeness instinctively. Only 3 percent of the contacts reported in the survey resembled the one most feared by parents, the adult stranger attempting to seduce a child.

Benjamin Radford, the managing editor of *Skeptical Inquirer* magazine, has noted instance after instance of the "one in five" figure and other kinds of misinformation on network TV broadcasts. On April 18, 2005, CBS reporter Jim Acosta declared on the evening news, "When a child is missing, chances are good it was a convicted sex offender." Radford responds, "Acosta is incorrect: if a child goes missing, a convicted sex offender is actually among the *least* likely explanations, far behind runaways, family abductions, and the child being lost or injured."

The undisputed champ of hyping child sexual predation is NBC reporter Chris Hansen, who has repeatedly warned Americans that "the scope of the problem is immense" and "growing." For several years Hansen hosted a popular series called "To Catch a Predator" on *Dateline NBC*. The show turned the moment of an alleged predator's confrontation and arrest into lurid home entertainment. In the opening episodes, Hansen reported that there were "fifty thousand" sexual predators preying on children through the Internet at any given moment. There was no good basis for the "fifty thousand" figure, and Hansen eventually stopped citing it. His source turned out to be an FBI agent named Ken Lanning, who told NPR's Brooke Gladstone that he didn't really know where the number came from but that it was familiar to him from another context. "In the early 1980s," he explained, chuckling, "this was the number that was most often used to estimate how many children were kidnapped or abducted by strangers every year. But the research that was done in the early 1990s found that somewhere in the neighborhood of two to three hundred children every year were abducted in this manner." Fifty thousand was "a Goldilocks number," Lanning said. "It wasn't a real small number—it wasn't like one hundred, two hundred—and it wasn't a ridiculously large number, like ten million. . . . [It was] not too hot, not too cold."

Like other popular delusions, fear of the Internet child molester contains a trace of logic. It is reasonable to ask whether the explosion of Internet pornography, including child pornography, might lead more troubled souls down a path to criminal depravity. But the Internet has been with us since the mid-1990s. If it were going to cause a sudden increase in molestation, wouldn't we have seen it by now? In fact, the trend lines go the opposite way. For instance, sexual assaults on teens fell dramatically—by 52 percent—between 1993 and 2005, according to the Justice Department's National Crime Victimization Survey.

Despite numbers like these, people are ready to believe there is an epidemic because they are repulsed by child pornography and assume that anyone who would look at it or think about it is not just perverted but dangerous. Those who take pictures of children engaged in sex acts and distribute them are criminals, and their actions have real victims. They are the most appropriate targets for law enforcement. There is no evidence that their sordid practices have bred an army of Internet predators.

In the preface of his classic nineteenth-century study, *Extraordinary Popular Delusions and the Madness of Crowds*, Charles Mackay wrote, "Men . . . go mad in herds, while they only recover their senses slowly, and one by one." Defeating this popular delusion is hard because almost no one has sympathy for an accused child molester. Evidence of the predilection alone is enough for many people to want a subject arrested and imprisoned. Who is going to complain loudly about a sicko being put behind bars or closely monitored, even if he has never acted on his desires? Law enforcement officials are not above turning this reality to their advantage.

But, as ever, belief trumps evidence.

The Justice Department program that supports Michele Deery's work consists today of fifty-nine investigative units

throughout the country. Last year alone they arrested more than
thirty-one hundred people like those on Deery's bulletin board.
The website for Deery's unit carries a curiously worded warn-
ing that is actually a tacit admission that there is no evidence
for its claim. It says that the problem of online child predation
"is growing so exponentially as to be impossible to track." In a
2006 speech at the National Center for Missing and Exploited
Children, then attorney general Alberto Gonzales managed to
strike both of this hysteria's most notorious false notes, citing
the one-in-five ratio and the fifty thousand figure. He concluded,
"It is simply astonishing how many predators there are, and how
aggressive they act."

Well, maybe not. Some of the dazed faces of arrested men
on Deery's bulletin board may be genuine predators, but it is
likely that most are simply troubled men with poor judgment
and oversexed imaginations. They find very little sympathy
before judges and juries. Yet, it's entirely possible that the greater
danger to society here is the police. Three researchers at the
University of New Hampshire reported earlier this year that
during the period between 2000 and 2006, when Internet use
by juveniles grew between 73 and 93 percent, the number of
people arrested for soliciting sex online from them grew only
21 percent, from 508 to 615. The number of people arrested for
soliciting sex from undercover police like Deery, however, rose
381 percent during the same period. In other words, alleged
child molesters like J are many, many times more likely to be
locked up for approaching detectives than children. And despite
this full-court press on Internet child predation, those arrested
for it represent only 1 percent of all arrests for sex crimes against
children and adolescents.

Some of the thirty-one hundred men arrested under the federal program may be genuine predators. With stern prison sentences in play, a lawyer defending an accused man is understandably hesitant to try an entrapment defense when prosecutors offer a plea deal to some lesser charge, with a relatively short period of imprisonment followed by treatment. Judges and juries have little sympathy for anyone who would entertain sex with a child, even as a fantasy, and detectives such as Deery are well schooled in the rules. After only his first conversation, J's legal case for entrapment was weak. In his opening line he listed "young" among his other sexual interests without any prompting. All Deery had asked was, "why don't u tell me wht ur into?" And if you read this initial conversation looking for evidence of predisposition, it was there aplenty. It would take a careful parsing of the dialogue, and a subtle understanding of the context, to conclude anything other than J's guilt.

His case illustrates just how slippery is the terrain. To the detective, J was a potential child molester. To J, he was a desperately horny man trying to arrange a sexual encounter.

As J tells it, theirs was a no-holds-barred erotic negotiation, something that had started as a game but that rapidly evolved into the possibility of a real-world assignation. J had read heather quickly and correctly: she was primarily interested in arranging for him to have sex with her girls. He wanted the sex with her, not with the daughters, but picked up quickly that the former could not be had without promises of the latter. So, as men have throughout time, he was prepared to pledge the one thing in order to get the other.

As Deery saw it, there were people who preyed sexually on children, and her job was to stop them. To find those people, she had to visit some very ugly virtual places, adopt some awful personas, and engage in highly distasteful conversations. The bad guys revealed themselves to her in her disguise. All she did was create an opportunity. She had not suggested having sex with her "daughters"—parafling had. His graphic scenarios were disgusting and damning, and sounded like the comments of someone intimately familiar with child rape. They had spilled out after only general prompting. As she saw it, this asshole was a dangerous predator. His insistence on meeting her alone before being introduced to the girls was, she believed, a ploy. TV shows like Hansen's had made the bad guys wary. He wanted to see her alone only to make sure she wasn't a cop before proceeding further.

The challenge would now be to avoid the request for a one-on-one encounter and get him to act directly on the sexual encounter with her imaginary girls, and to lure him into the open.

Heather had asked J a question:

—*u ever playd w yung?*

J was ready to play that game with her, to engage in her fantasy in order to set her up for what he wanted: a chance to meet and have sex with her alone. To make that happen, he would become the perfect answer to her dark wish. So he lied to her. He told her he had once licked the vagina of a nine-year-old girl. She responded:

—*k*

After reassuring her on that count, J immediately came back with the scenario he preferred.

—I am looking to have you first then you and the girls or
any way you feel comfortable. We would go as far as you
want on any level
—so ur not new 2 this
—been 10 years or more but i will get back in the groove, lol
—lol

She asked about his marriage, and J told her, "she is into
NOTHING at all I mean NOTHING. she knows nothing about
me like this."
He wrote:

—so all we do willbe between you and I baby
—cool w me
—OH I will get out I drive all day long I could meet you
during the day too even if girls were not there
—they get hm by 3 school is rite dwn the street

J saw the pattern. Every time he mentioned having sex with
her alone, she would bring back the girls—"they get hm by 3."
He could work with that:

—then at evening or weekend can please you and girls,
shades drawn ... could do you in AM then back for them,
lol I can be flexaable darling
—ur pretty creative

If he could get her alone they could play, and he would be
long gone by the time she came home with the girls. That could
work. Real sex! He was tremendously excited by the idea.

—I have thought about this for so long baby
—yea its been a while for them

Them. "OK," he thought. "I get it." At this point J plunged in, inventing a sexual encounter with her and the girls, giving heather exactly what he thought she was after. The details were so graphic they were grotesque. This kind of sex talk was not completely new to him. He had engaged other women online within the last few weeks with highly descriptive talk about sex with their children. So he asked specific questions about how physically able the girls were to have sex, and then slid back onto his own erotic turf, asking her if she liked to be tied up or to have clamps applied to her nipples. She wrote three successive lines:

—not so much no
—depends i guess
—how did u get into yung? u grow up in it too?

Back to the girls. Clearly this was a fixation with her. This was the itch she wanted scratched, no doubt about it. J ran with it. In his fantasies, there were no boundaries he was unwilling to cross. He would play her game because the prospect of meeting her in real life and having real sex had suddenly become the compelling drive of his life. It was a must. He conjured an especially lurid scenario that involved his deflowering a child. She responded:

—nice

Running bizarrely with the fantasy, J wrote:

—I know you cannot but I love the idea of breeding a mom,
and in time doing my own daugter with you
—u seem like a for real dude

J set about trying again to arrange a rendezvous with her alone, suggesting mornings, when the girls were in school. She balked. She reminded him they did not get off school until three o'clock, writing:

—*IM SO not a am person lol. im a night owl*

J pushed:

—*maybe you will want your lover to yourself some times, lol*

She brushed aside the idea:

—*lol*

When he persisted with the idea of a morning romp, just the two of them, she grew adamant:

—*im NOT A MORNING PERSON DEAR not my thing*

And J backed off:

—*ok as you wish*

She asked him again to describe what he wanted, and he unfolded a scene where he would watch the three of them, mother and children, playing sexually with one another.

—*so ur more into watchin?*

Uh-oh. He could lose her with this.

—*NO want to see that and as you all are doing things i wil
be doing things too but love to see that*
—*ok*

J heard his wife opening the front door, and quickly shut down the computer. He didn't have time to sign off. Four times later that night he wrote lines to heather, whenever he would see her name on the list of active participants on his screen. He apologized for signing off without saying goodbye, explained, and reiterated his interest. At 10:36 that night he wrote "HI baby," but there was no response. He tried once more at 1:01 a.m., with a hopeful, "HI baby hope we can talk agin::."

No answer.

J's plaintive "HI baby hope we can talk agin::" entered just after one in the morning, hung there on the screen until he gave up and finally went to bed. He found her reassuring answer in the morning.

—*no biggie.. just lemme know when ur around*

J pounced on the response immediately, in a froth of desire.

—*I want you so fucking badly PLEASE hold*

His wife was on her way out the door. J left the screen for a few minutes and then came raging back with a graphic description of the various sexual acts he would like to perform with heather alone. Her response was skeptical:

—*o?*

J regrouped:

—*you dont want that darling BUT you know what I really want?????*
—*what?*
—*to please you and please your daughters*

He offered to come by and see her that day, and launched again into a litany of sexual acts he was eager to perform with her. He suggested that when they had finished she might show him pictures of her daughters. This prompted a complaint:

—*ur flip floppin its confusing me ... i mean it just seems like ur more into me then all of us..thats all*

There it was, the deal again. J backtracked fast.

—*NO NO,,,,,,, want to please you first and get the ball rolling that is all it will be hard to be with you and them all, for the first time that is all i am saying would like to have you first then i will have the girls over and over YUMMMMMMMMMMMMM*

And so the negotiation proceeded for the next month. She would back off whenever he talked about having sex with her alone, so he would indulge her, conjure up more graphic scenes of sex with her and the girls, but always he would return to his preferred plan for their real-world rendezvous. And consistently she would steer him right back to the daughters.

—*what should i tell the girls is what i really wanna know?*

When he persisted in asking her to describe herself, she complained:

—*your annoying me now*

After weeks of this, down in her basement cubicle at the courthouse, Deery was at an impasse. It wouldn't do to arrange a meeting with parafling without her "girls." There was no crime in arranging a kinky sex session with an adult woman. The meeting had to be on his terms, and if what he wanted was just to have sex with her, all he had to do was admit it,

and she would drop her investigation. She kept offering him
the door out.

> —ok i understand i think .. whatever u want .. its up to you
> —well I would LIKE to meet you make love to you, then
> return to take your girls, with you there. like the senerio we
> spoke about,,,,, that is what I would like,,,,, just need you
> to be ok with that
> —ill think about it .. that just seems kinda weird to me ill let
> u know ... just seems odd to me that you woudl want to come
> here to do me .. then come back to do them .. seems shady

She had put her finger precisely on J's game. He intended
to show up, have sex with heather, and then split, but if she
suspected that, he knew his opportunity would disappear. He
poured cold water all over that suggestion:

> —shady?? really,,, WOW well it is NOT NOT at all,,, just
> a comfort level thing NOTHING shady at all ,,,,,,,,,

Heather drifted away. The next day she gave him a series of
one-word responses. Then she was gone for days. On Wednesday of the following week they again began trying to work out a
rendezvous and again got hung up over his desire to meet with
her alone. She complained:

> —u say ur not really just into me, but it is still odd to me
> that you just wanna meet ME..
> —ok allow me to explain, ok,,,, as i told you before it was
> only a comfort level,,,,, all 3 hot woman all new, might me
> overwhelming and way HOT, lol so I only SUGGESTED
> to meet you first for a comfort level thing,,,,,,,,,,,

Whenever he went back to talking about sex with her daughters, heather would warm to the dialogue. After outlining one such imaginary encounter, he asked her:

—*and you will like that too???, me playing with you and them???*

She wrote:

—*when they r happy i am too that's why i said it seemed lk u were into me n not them.. if that's the case thats cool.. just say that no biggie*
—*NO into ALL want ALL*
—*k*
—*but if I can meet and play sometimes when the goirls are NOT home, we can still play right, I want all when ever I can, you, you and the girl, just the girls, what ever*
—*ok thats fair*

They made plans to meet the next day, and then J launched into another explicit fantasy of how sex between her and the girls together would go. Heather encouraged him to continue, interjecting:

—*I like how creative u r*

and

—*tell me*

and, referring to an explicitly described sex act with her eleven-year-old,

—*she will like that*

and

—*then what*

Except that, revealingly, she noticed that the fantasy he was spinning did not include him. He was the watcher, as she played sexually with the girls. No crime there, at least on his part. She would be the main actor. She complained:

> —*here is a tidbit of info ... i can do all that w out you here ... so clearly you are more into me then all of us whch is fine but u should be upfront about that from the get go*

J tried to recover, but she retreated, writing:

> —*just sounds kinda off to me i gotta go .. tt u later*

She was gone.

This was the pattern their dialogue assumed for another month. J was on the line looking for heather every morning and evening. He followed the same routine he had for years. He would log on in the morning before he left for work, then in the evening when he got home, and then again at night, when he would turn on the TV—that was his cover, just watching the tube—and then slide over to the chair before his computer cabinet and reenter his fantasy realm. If he heard footsteps on the stairs he would quickly close the cabinet doors over the screen and jump back to the couch in front of the TV. But once his wife went upstairs, she usually didn't come back down.

Again and again J would propose an actual meeting between himself and heather—she told him that was really her middle name, which she used online. His repeated efforts to engage her in a discussion of adult sex and to focus on the sex acts they would perform alone were gently but persistently rebuffed.

When he kept asking her to describe herself, she complained:

—*your annoying me now*

And she would stop responding. This was not what she wanted. After one such exchange, J typed:

—*ok I guess your not talking to me now, it is cool, don't worry about it we will talk some other time,,,,,,,,,,,,,,, you have a great day*

She repeated again and again that her girls came home from school at three, and just as stubbornly J kept trying to arrange to see her before then. When he abandoned efforts to arrange a morning tryst, he started pushing to meet with her an hour before the girls got out of school, promising to come back another time to meet the girls. On the morning of September 22, he wrote:

—*what time, 1:30 ish to meet and make love to you or 2 what works best*
—*2 is actually better*
—*and the girls get there at 3*
—*yea*
—*ok we will play fast then*
—*but ur comin back tomorrow rite?*
—*just want you and I not to scare them, LOL*
—*how would we scare them?*
—*walking in to you and I fucking*
—*lol come on now*
—*LOL tits tied with zip cords, LOL*

—that won't scare them goof
—and do you have handcuffs

The detective must have gotten a real-world chuckle out of that question. But this guy definitely posed a problem. An assignation with a grown woman was hardly a crime. He was promising to drive out on Friday, September 23, to meet her, but she was not content with the timing. She wanted him to push the time back, which would enable her to provide a frame for the meeting that would be incriminating. At the later time, "the girls" were off school. She wrote:

—so ur comin tomorrow 2? Just don't wanna think ur just into me n not them.. kinda getting that vibe
—OH NO don't think that, that would be a mistake baby just need you first THEN them
—ok

If he was going to come to meet with her alone, she would like to have some evidence that he planned to stick around for criminal sex with the girls.

—girls like presents lol bring us presents lol u been thinkn bout this a lot huh?
—I told you I want ALL
—ok just checkin
—we will talk today about presents to bring them baby
—k

She gave him her phone number during that Thursday-morning conversation. J called her six times in the next twelve hours. She did not answer. On Friday morning he typed a note of greeting to her and got no response. She wrote him back hours later when he was out doing his rounds. She sounded peeved.

> —sorry., I got stuck at home w work … n I worked last night 2.. anyway.. givin u my number was 2 call to meet up not 2 call all hours of the day/night. I guess that gave me a bad vibe as 2 who u really r n ur real interests in me/us…, we r goin 2 the shore w a friend this weekend n wont be back til sun nite have good weekend

He found her note when he got home early from work that afternoon. Chastened, he tried to patch things up.

> —well sorry about your vibe, because it was a wrong vibe,,,, I will not call til you tell me too, I tried to call to hook up yesterday and today,,,,,, my interest is in your girls but I did want to meet you first, so I was trying to hook up with you, so the next time and the future would be with them,,,, I am sorry you felt like that, because it is NOT a correct one, yes I want to hook up with you first but then then, I was only trying to get us all started, that was all,, so I will NOT call your number again, UNTIL you tell me to hook up again, OK???? I hope we can do this next week and I hope we can talk again … I do want as you put it, US,,, you me and the girls and I would love to babysit for you too some time, LOL again have a good weekend and we will talk on Monday

He did not hear from her for another week. Each day he would type apologetic messages to her and get no response. When she reappeared the following Friday afternoon, J was desperate to right things. He rushed pathetically to reassure her that he was on board with her fantasy completely, even dangling

the possibility of a sex session with the girls first, but then immediately retreated from it:

> —hey question, would you like me to by pass you, and just
> have the girls. I do not want to worry you that I only wanted
> you,,,, if you would like me to have them only I can do, you
> need to tell me what your ok with
> —that's why i asked ... u what ur into b/c i wasn't sure.
> —that is totally cool ... I wanted you first then the girls ...
> just it would make it easier on me when I am there with you
> and them, you and I would have already been together and
> I would feel a lot more comfortable with them, then, but if
> you would prefer that I do NOT play with you and have
> only them, I can do, but I really wanted all of you

The meeting had to be on *his* terms, and if what he wanted
was just to have sex with her, all he had to do was admit it, and she
would drop her investigation. She kept offering him the door out.

> —ok I understand I think ... whatever u want ... its up
> to you
> —well I would LIKE to meet you make love to you, then
> return to take your girls with you there, like the scenario we
> spoke about,,,, that is what I would like,,,, just need you to
> be ok with that
> —ill think about it ... that just seems kinda weird to me ill
> let u know ... it just seems odd to me that you would want
> to come here to do me ... then come back to do them ...
> seems shady

Through the rest of October, heather would disappear for
days at a time, emerge just for a perfunctory exchange, and then

disappear again. For J, the breakthrough came on the afternoon of Monday, October 24, when for the first time she agreed to his scenario of meeting her alone for sex first. His proposal had not changed:

> —*I was just thinking maybe you and I could meet earlier,,,,,*
> *play, I will wait in your bed as you leave and get the girl and*
> *then send in the oldest, when i will be in bed naked you close*
> *the door wait outside with youngest*
> —*thats cool*

After more detailing of the various sexual acts planned with both her and the girls, again rendered in explicit detail, J reiterated:

> —*... so we will play fast then if i get there at 2 since you need*
> *to pich the gorls up at 3 wow ok, fast one I see that is cool*
> —*why do u keep askin me that? to come here then leave*
> *then come back? seems odd*
> —*NO I am just trying to make it easy on ALL nothing*
> *sneaking at all*
> —*huh?*
> —*I am coolith whatever you ewant*
> —*well what do you want? im open after 2 .. i told u that a*
> *million times*
> —*ok cool*
> —*seems like ur really not into the girls, if not just say that*
> *.. its all good either way*

Again J assured her that he was interested in her *and* her girls, but once more he made it clear that he was coming to meet her alone first. They would have sex and then she would leave to get the girls. After weeks of wrangling, heather had finally agreed to what he wanted.

Deery relented. It wasn't as clean as she might have liked, but she had him. They arranged to rendezvous on the afternoon of Friday, October 28, in the parking lot of a Wendy's on MacDade Boulevard just outside of Media. She asked J to bring condoms, and he promised to do so. But at the last moment he panicked.

On the morning of their meeting, J wrote heather:

> —*I had a fucked up dream last night, lol*
> —*do tell?*
> —*that you set me up like you were the cops, I walked in and you arrested me for this and I needed to kill myself, because I will never go to jail lol*
> —*good god! are u serious*
> —*I know … freaked me out*

She reassured him. Before they signed off that morning, J made sure one more time that the plan was the way he wanted it. He would meet her, they would have sex, and then she would leave to pick up her girls and come back with them.

> —*do they know I will have you first too??*

For J, it was a short drive along Interstate 476, the Blue Route, to MacDade Boulevard. Before heading for their rendezvous he showered and changed into casual slacks, dress shoes, and a clean gray pullover shirt. He turned off the expressway and pointed northeast on the busy four-lane highway, lined on both sides by strip malls. He was excited. His persistence had paid off. Heather had described herself to him as Italian, dark-eyed, dark-haired, and he had a vivid mental picture of her submitting herself to him that made his heart pound. He had purchased the condoms she requested at a Rite Aid, a three-pack, the smallest item on the rack. He had the condoms in a bag with the sex toys he hoped to use in the short time they had before she would leave to get her daughters. In the bag was a set of handcuffs, just the play kind with no locks on them, some dildos, and some rope, in case she wanted to be tied up. He wanted to be right on time, because there would be only an hour for them to get to her house and have sex before she had to leave to get her daughters—and then he would flee.

He crossed through a wide intersection, turned into the restaurant parking lot, and started backing into a space. A car startled him, pulling up fast, right behind him, cutting him off. It made him angry, but then he saw another had pulled in front of him. They had nearly hit his car! Then men rushed toward him with handguns drawn. They were shouting, "Get out of the car! Get out of the car!"

His first thought was that it was a holdup. He was being robbed or carjacked. But then one of the men told him he was under arrest. These were cops. He stepped out and was immediately pushed against the side of his car and frisked, handcuffed, and placed in the back of a sport-utility vehicle. Deery was watching from her own car nearby. She did not get out.

J moved like someone in shock. Lieutenant David Peifer, Deery's boss and head of the ICAC unit, got behind the wheel. He was about J's age, a sturdy man with a crew cut and a handgun on his belt. J flung questions at him. Why was he being arrested? Because he had come there to meet with a woman?

The lieutenant told him, in so many words, that he was under arrest for "soliciting" sex with children.

"I would never have touched those kids!" J protested. "I wasn't interested in them!"

"That's what they all say," Peifer replied.

J kept trying to explain himself, and the lieutenant told him, patiently, that he had to wait until they got back to his office, where they could talk at length. First he had to be fully advised of his rights.

His rights! J was angry, bewildered, and frightened. He knew that the scenario he had described to heather online was criminal, and he had seen busts like this on TV, but somehow his knowledge that the fantasies he described were untrue, that he never intended for them to actually happen, had convinced him he was safe. How could meeting an adult woman alone make him vulnerable to arrest?

He met Deery for the first time at the police station. He was sitting on a bench in Peifer's office, feeling vulnerable and foolish, his thick arms resting in his lap, handcuffed to a chair. When the detective entered and sat down, J didn't know who she was until the lieutenant introduced her as "Heather." She seemed timid. Peifer did most of the talking. J was frightened but also angry. He tried to stay calm as he explained to them both that he'd had no intention, despite whatever he had written, of sticking around for sex with the girls. Deery said, "You brought three condoms, one for me and one for each of the girls."

"They come in packs of three," he told her. "You can't buy just one."

Still, that looked bad.

Peifer set a microcassette recorder in the desk and read him his rights, and J then reviewed a form explaining that he was entitled to have a lawyer present, that he had been read the Miranda warnings, and that he was waiving them all, agreeing to answer questions. He didn't just agree, he was *frantic* to explain himself, to explain it all away. Both Peifer and Deery signed as witnesses to the statement.

J answered Peifer's questions about where he lived, where he kept his computer, his log-ins and passwords. He told them they would find some porn on his computer, files that had been e-mailed to him.

"There's a few snapshots," he said. "It's not that I keep them, but they were sent years ago. . . . But I didn't go out and search it. I did not do child pornography. I never search anything like that."

Peifer and Deery gave J a transcript of the chats he had had with heatherscutiepies and started reading to him some of the more explicit things he had said about having sex with children. J was frantic to explain himself. "The conversations were based on just to keep the woman interested and to just be erotic and aroused, and that was it," he said. They were not buying it. Peifer read him line after embarrassing, incriminating line.

"I, honest to God . . . ," said J, exasperated. "I don't want them [the girls]. I never been into it, ever with anybody, anywhere, at any time!"

"And that's easy to say now that we've arrested you, and you're sitting here talking to the police," said Peifer.

"Even if I wasn't arrested, I wouldn't be interested in kids. It was just, I wanted . . . the woman to be excited. I wanted *me* to be excited. And that was it. I know how it looks. I know what you're reading, but—"

"When you bring kids into this whole thing, why would you even go there?" asked Peifer.

"I know," J said, defeated, but still trying to make them see, running phrases together in his panic. "The idea was only to keep her interested. I, in my mind, my mind, was working differently, I guess, than most people's, because I just wanted to be with a real woman, not the kids, but I wanted, I didn't want to lose my opportunity to, to have some real passion, and I, I was wrong in stating that. I know you're telling me it's solicitation, in your definition, but I, I can tell you that when I was doing it, it's not solicit—I wasn't trying to solicit because I know in my heart and in my mind, I would not under any circumstances be with a child and nor have I ever, ever, ever, in any way shape or form, been with a child. I never want to."

"But you'd never know that by reading this chat," said Peifer.

"I understand that," said J.

It went on like this. He could see how they viewed what he had written, and it was obvious that it looked very bad. It would look that way to anyone who didn't understand. It looked *criminal*.

"I have no interest in young kids, whatsoever," J insisted. "It was just cyber chat, to be a lie, and to try and keep the mother interested so I could have some passion with an older woman, which I've missed at home."

"But it doesn't stay cyber chat when you get in your car, and you drive from Exton to Delaware County and park at the Wendy's parking lot waiting for the mom and the two kids," said Peifer.

"The mom was going to get the kids after we had, had sex, and then, when she left, I was leaving. I was not going to have sex with the kids."

"That's what you say now."

"That's what I would say now and yesterday and the day before that."

"No, no, no, no," said Deery. "What you said yesterday was when the mom leaves to go get the kids, you were going to wait in her bed naked, and the oldest daughter was to be sent into that bedroom."

"That was written, yes."

"That was what was said yesterday," said Deery.

"That is correct, but that is no—"

"And the day before."

"But that is not what I was planning on doing, that was only to keep your interest."

"OK, again, that's self-serving now that you're under arrest."

"Even if I wasn't under arrest, I would feel the same way."

When they were finished, J asked Peifer when he could go home.

He still did not understand the seriousness of his predicament.

"No," the lieutenant explained in the calm, patient way of his. "You're being arrested, and you are going to jail tonight."

J served a year in prison. His lawyer negotiated a plea that reduced what might have been a much longer stay, and that allowed him to serve his time in a relatively unthreatening county prison. He was charged with sixteen counts, starting with "criminal attempt—rape forcible compulsion" and ending with "criminal solicitation—corruption of minors." He was

given one year of parole and sentenced to ten years of probation, during which time he must attend counseling weekly
for his supposed sexual desire for children. His wife left him.
He lost his job. His face, name, address, and criminal conviction for "Attempted Involuntary Sexual Deviate Intercourse"
with a minor appear on the Pennsylvania website for "sexual
offenders," the modern equivalent of a scarlet letter. There it
will remain until 2016.

He is deeply ashamed, and bitter. He wanted to fight the
charge. Indeed, he is still furious with the lawyer who persuaded
him to take a plea, but it would appear that the copy-machine
repairman received wise counsel. Because he didn't have a
prayer of getting off. The array of charges against him could
have sent him away to prison for up to eight years. At the trial,
he would have been painted as an all-too-familiar monster. This
was the interpretation of Deery and the Delaware County district attorney, and they were not particularly interested in any
other. They might have been able to find out for sure on the
day they arrested him. Deery could have worn a wire, and if he
had been as determined as she believed he was to have sex with
her daughters, she could have presented him with that exact
opportunity, telling him, for example, that her girls were home
at that moment and she was going to take him directly there,
bypassing the prospect of his having sex with her. It might have
unequivocally sorted out his interests. But it was clear that, to
her, such a consideration was moot.

"I had enough already to convict him," she said. "There was
no need for a wire."

J was guilty of some things, serious things. He was guilty of
saying he wanted to have sex with two imaginary children. He

was guilty of being a troubled soul in a bad marriage, of abusing steroids, of a lifelong inability to establish a healthy intimacy with a woman, and of being morally adrift in a netherworld of illicit sexual desire. He was guilty of lacking moral boundaries and good sense. There is a chance that without treatment of some kind, J would have evolved into someone dangerous. I asked him, "What if you found yourself, after all of that talk on the Internet, consumed with your steroidal lust, in a room with this woman and her children? Is it possible that you might have gone ahead with it?"

J bowed his head and thought about it for a long time.

"I don't know," he said. "I know I have no sexual interest in children at all. I pray that I would never have gone that far. I certainly had no intention of doing it. I intended to have sex with her and then leave. Period."

There is no evidence that J has ever made a sexual over-ture to a child. Deery told me that she couldn't remember ever arresting a child molester who did not have child porn on his computer. It is all too easy to obtain. J had no images that were obviously child porn. His appalled parents paid for a battery of psychosexual testing, the kind where involuntary responses to images are measured. The tests showed exactly what J claimed, that he had no sexual interest in children.

J is off steroids. His body has slipped back into a normal slightly pudgy shape. His manner is subdued, submissive, ear-nest, eagerly friendly, and polite. He helped several inmates earn high school diplomas when he was in jail, and he is proud of that. He no longer owns a computer. He lives alone in his suburban town house with his dogs. He has joined a church. He says the pastor there has embraced him, forgiven him, and provided him with support and direction. After his arrest he went to every neighbor in his suburban cul-de-sac, knocking on doors to tell each of them his story. He did not want them to know only what they learned from the police. He says they believe him, and he feels accepted. He recently found a new job, after telling his whole story to the man who hired him. He sees the years he spent obsessed with cybersex as an illness, or a lapse into sinfulness, that drew him deeper and deeper into depravity. He is embarrassed. He has been humiliated.

But he has stayed angry. The classes he attends as a condition of his probation demand that he admit a sexual desire for children. It is considered an essential step toward recovery. J told his instructor that he has no such desire. He never did. He was told that if he persists in this denial he will jeopardize his probation and could be sent back to jail.

So he pretends to be something he is not. He is good at it.

The Case of the Vanishing Blonde

Vanity Fair, December 2010

From the start, it was a bad case.

A battered twenty-one-year-old woman with long blonde curls was discovered facedown in the weeds, naked, at the western edge of Miami, where the neat grid of outer suburbia butts up against the high grass and black mud of the Everglades. It was early on a winter morning in 2005. A local power-company worker was driving by the empty lots of an unbuilt cul-de-sac when he saw her.

And much to his surprise, she was alive. She was still unconscious when the police airlifted her to Jackson Memorial Hospital. When she woke up in its trauma center, she could remember little about what had happened to her, but her body told an ugly tale. She had been raped, badly beaten, and left for dead. There was severe head trauma; she had suffered brain-rattling blows. Semen was recovered from inside her. The bones around her right eye were shattered. She was terrified and confused. She bent English to her native Ukrainian grammar and syntax, drop-ping pronouns and inverting standard sentence structure, which made her hard to understand. And one of the first things she asked for on waking was her lawyer. That was unusual.

Miami-Dade detectives learned that Inna Budnytska had been living for months at the Airport Regency Hotel, eight miles from where she was found. It is one of those crisply effi-cient overnight spots in the orbit of major airports that cater to travelers needing a bed between legs of long flights. She was employed by a cruise-ship line and had severely cut her finger on the job, so she was being put up at the hotel by her employers while she healed. The assault had begun, she said, in her room on the fourth floor. She described her attackers as two or three white men who spoke with accents she heard as "Hispanic," but she wasn't certain. She remembered one of the men push-ing a pillow into her face, and being forced to drink something strong, alcoholic. Inna had fragments of memories like bits of a bad dream—of being held up or carried, of being thrown over a man's shoulder as he moved down a flight of stairs, of being roughly violated in the back seat of a car, of pleading for her life. Powerful, cruel moments, but there was nothing solid, nothing that made a decent lead. When her lawyer soon after filed a law-suit against the hotel, alleging negligence, going after potentially deep corporate pockets, the detectives thought something was fishy. This was not your typical rape victim. What if she was part of some sophisticated con?

The police detectives did what they could at the hotel, comb-ing Inna's room for evidence, interviewing hotel employees, obtaining images from all of the surveillance cameras for the morning of the crime, going over the guest lists. The hotel had

174 rooms, and so many people came and went that it would
have taken months working full-time to run checks on every one
of them—something beyond the resources of a police department in a high-crime area like Miami-Dade. The sex-crimes
unit set aside the file with no clear leads, only more questions.
After several weeks, "we were dried up," recalled Allen Foote,
the detective handling the case.

So the action was all headed toward civil court. The hotel
engaged a law firm to defend itself from the woman's lawsuit,
and the firm eventually hired a private detective named Ken
Brennan to figure out what had happened.

Foote was not pleased. It was usually a pain in the ass to have
a private detective snooping around one of his cases. Brennan
was right out of central casting—middle-aged, deeply tanned,
with gray hair. He was a weight lifter and favored open-necked
shirts that showed off both the definition of his upper pecs and
the bright, solid-gold chain around his neck. The look said:
mature, virile, laid-back, and making it. He had been divorced,
and his former wife was now deceased; his children were grown.
He had little in the way of daily family responsibilities. Brennan
had been a cop on Long Island, where he was from, and had
worked for eight years as an agent for the Drug Enforcement
Administration (DEA). He had left the agency in the mid-90s
to work as a commodities broker and to set up as a private detective. The brokering was not to his taste, but the investigating was.
He was a warm, talkative guy, with a thick Long Island accent,
who sized people up quickly and with a healthy strain of New
York brass. If he liked you, he let you know it right away, and you
were his friend for life, and if he didn't . . . well, you would find
that out right away too. Nothing shocked him; in fact, most

of the salacious run-of-the-mill work that pays private detectives' bills—domestic jobs and petty insurance scams—bored him. Brennan turned those offers away. The ones he took were mostly from businesses and law firms who hired him to nail down the facts in civil court cases, like this one.

He had a fixed policy. He told potential employers up front, "I'll find out what happened. I'm not going to shade things to assist your client, but I will find out what the truth is." Brennan liked it when the information he uncovered helped his clients, but that wasn't a priority. Winning lawsuits wasn't the goal. What excited him was the mystery.

The job in this case was straightforward. Find out who raped and beat this young woman and dumped her in the weeds. Had the attack even happened at the hotel, or had she slipped out and met her assailant or assailants someplace else? Was she just a simple victim, or was she being used by some kind of Eastern European syndicate? Was she a prostitute? Was she somehow implicated? There were many questions and few answers.

"I used to be a cop and a federal agent," Brennan told Detective Foote, introducing himself at the offices of the Miami-Dade police sex-crimes unit. Foote had long, strawberry-blond hair, which he combed straight back, and a bushy blond mustache. He was about the same age as Brennan, who read him right away as a fellow member of the fraternity, somebody he could reason with on familiar terms.

"Look, you and I both know there's no fucking way you can investigate this case," Brennan said. "I can see this through to the end. I won't step on your dick. I won't do a thing without telling you about it. If I figure out who did it, you get the arrest. I won't do anything to fuck it up for you."

Foote saw logic in this and did something he ordinarily wouldn't do; he shared what he had in his file: crime-scene photos, surveillance footage from the hotel security cameras, the victim's confused statement. Foote had interviewed several hotel staff members, but they hadn't seen a thing. He'd gone about as far as he could with it. He thought, "Good luck."

The insurance adjuster had fared no better than Foote. As Brennan reviewed the adjuster's detailed summary of the case in early November 2005, eight months after Inna Budnytska had been found, it was easy to see why. Her memory was all over the map. First she said she had been attacked by one man, then three, then two. At one point she said their accent might have been not "Hispanic" but "Romanian." There was no evidence to implicate anyone.

The hotel had a significant security system. The property was fenced, and the back gates were locked and monitored. There were only a few points of entry and exit. During the night, the back door was locked and could be opened only remotely. There were two security guards on duty at all times. Each exit was equipped with a surveillance camera. There was one over the front entrance and one over the back, one in the lobby, one at the lobby elevator, and others out by the pool and the parking lot. All the hotel guests had digital key cards that left a computer record every time they unlocked the door to their rooms. It was possible to track the comings and goings of every person who checked in.

Brennan started where all good detectives start. What did he know for sure? He knew Inna Budnytska had gone up to her fourth-floor room at the Airport Regency at 3:41 a.m., that she had used her key card to enter her room at about the same time, and that she had been found at dawn in the weeds eight miles west. Somewhere in that roughly three-hour window, she had left the hotel. But there was no evidence of this on any of the cameras. So, how?

Inna was colorfully present on the video record, with her bright red puffy jacket and shoulder-length blonde curls. She had been in and out all night. After months of living in the hotel, she was clearly restless. She made frequent trips down to the lobby just to chat with hotel workers and guests, or to step outside for a smoke, and the cameras caught her every trip. She had gone out to dinner with a friend and returned around midnight, but she wasn't done yet. She is seen exiting the elevator at about three in the morning, and the camera over the front entrance catches her walking away. She told investigators that she had walked to a nearby gas station to buy a phone card, because she wanted to call her mother back in Ukraine, where people were just waking up. Minutes after her departure, the camera catches her return. The lobby camera records her reentering the hotel and crossing the lobby. Moments later she is seen entering the elevator for her final trip upstairs. A large black man gets onto the elevator right behind her, and the recording shows them exchanging a few words. The police report showed her entering her room twenty minutes later, which had led to much speculation about where she was during that time. Inna had no memory of going anywhere but directly to her room. Brennan had checked the clock on the elevator camera and found that it ran more than twenty minutes behind the computer clock, which recorded the key swipes, solving that small mystery. After she entered the lobby elevator, she was not seen again by any of the cameras.

All the surveillance cameras were in perfect working order. They were not on continually; they were activated by motion detectors. Miami-Dade detectives had even tried to beat the motion detectors by moving very slowly, or finding angles of approach that would not be seen, but they had failed. No matter how slowly they moved, no matter what approach they tried, the cameras clicked on faithfully and caught them.

One possibility was that she had left through her fourth-floor window. Someone would have had to drop her out the window or somehow lower her, presumably unconscious, into the bushes below, and then exit the hotel and walk around to retrieve her. But Inna showed no signs of injury from such a drop, or marks from ropes, and the bushes behind the hotel had not been trampled. The police had examined them carefully, looking for any sign of disturbance or blood. It was also possible, with more than one assailant, that she had been lowered into the grasp of someone who had avoided disturbing the bushes, but Brennan saw that such explanations began to severely stretch credulity. Sex crimes are not committed by determined teams of attackers who come with padded ropes to lower victims from fourth-floor windows.

No, Brennan concluded. Unless this crime had been pulled off by a team of magicians, the victim had to have come down in the elevator to the lobby and left through the front door. The answer was not obvious, but it had to be somewhere in the video record from those cameras. "Needless to say, the big mystery here is how this woman got out of the hotel," read the summary of the case prepared by the insurance adjuster. It was a mystery he had not been able to crack.

Brennan penciled one word on the memo: "Disguise?"

He began studying the video record with great care, until he could account for every coming and going. Whenever a person or a group arrived, the camera over the front door recorded it. Seconds later, the entries were captured by the lobby cameras, and then, soon after, by the elevator cameras. Room key records showed the arrivals entering their rooms. Likewise, those departing were recorded in the opposite sequence: elevator, lobby, front door. The parking-lot cameras recorded cars coming and going. One by one, Brennan eliminated scores of potential suspects. If someone had left the hotel before Inna reentered her room, and did not return, he could not have attacked her. Such people were eliminated. Those who entered and were not seen to leave were also eliminated, and likewise anyone exiting the hotel without a bag, or carrying only a small bag. Brennan eliminated no one without a clear reason, not even women or families. He watched carefully for any sign of someone behaving nervously or erratically.

This painstaking process ultimately left him with only one suspect: the man seen entering the elevator behind the victim at 3:41 a.m. He was a very large black man with glasses, who looked to be at least six foot four and upward of three hundred pounds. He and Inna are seen casually talking as they enter the elevator. The same man emerges from the elevator into the lobby less than two hours later, at 5:28 a.m., pulling a suitcase with wheels. The camera over the front door records him rolling the suitcase out toward the parking lot at a casual stroll. He returns less than an hour later, shortly before dawn, without the bag. He gets back on the elevator and heads upstairs.

Why would a man haul his luggage out of an airport hotel early in the morning, when he was not checking out, and then return to his room within the hour without it? That question, coupled with Brennan's careful process of elimination, led him to the conclusion that Budnytska had been taken out of the hotel inside the big man's suitcase.

But it seemed too small. It looked to be about the size that air travelers can fit into overhead compartments. However, the man himself was so big, perhaps the apparent size of the bag was an illusion. Brennan studied the video as the man exited the elevator and also as he left the hotel, then measured the doorways of both. When he matched visible reference points in the video—the number of tiles to each side of the bag as it was wheeled out the front door, and the height of the bar that ran around the inside of the elevator—he was able to get a close approximation of the suitcase's actual size. He obtained one that fit those measurements, which was larger than the bag on the video had appeared to be, and invited a flexible young woman whose proportions matched Inna's to curl up inside it. She fit.

He scrutinized the video still more closely, watching it again and again. The man steps off the elevator rolling the bag behind him. As he does, the wheels catch momentarily in the space between the elevator floor and the lobby floor, just for a split second. It was hardly noticeable if you weren't looking for it. The man has to give the bag a tug to get it unstuck.

And that clinched it. That tiny tug. The bag had to have been heavy to get stuck. Brennan was now convinced. This was the guy. No matter what Inna Budnytska had said—that she had been attacked by two or maybe three men, that they were "white," that they spoke with accents that sounded "Hispanic" or perhaps "Romanian"—Brennan was convinced her attacker had to be this man. Her head injuries had left her very confused about the night, and the language barrier could also account for some of the confusion about her answers.

The detective was struck by something else. His suspect was entirely collected. Cool and calm, entering the elevator with the woman, exiting with the suitcase, pulling it behind him out to the parking lot, then strolling back in less than an hour later. Brennan had been a cop. He had seen ordinary men caught up in the aftermath of a violent crime. They were beside themselves. Shaking. Panicky. If a man rapes and beats a woman to the point where he thinks she's dead, and then hauls the body out to dump it in the weeds, does he come strolling back into the same hotel as if nothing happened? An ordinary attacker would have been two states away by noon.

What this big man's demeanor suggested to Brennan was chilling.

He's good at this. He's done this before.

Brennan called a meeting at the hotel on November 17, 2005. The hotel owners were there, the insurance adjusters, and the lawyers—in other words, the people who had hired him. They met in a boardroom. On a laptop screen, Brennan pulled up the image of the large man pulling his suitcase off the elevator.

He said, "This is the guy that did it. That girl is inside that suitcase."

There was some snickering.

"How do you come up with that?' he was asked. Brennan described his process of elimination, how he had narrowed and narrowed the search until it led him to this man.

They weren't buying it.

"Didn't the victim say that she was attacked by two white guys?" one of them asked.

"I'm telling you," said Brennan. "This is the guy. Let me run with it a little bit. If you're willing to give me the resources, I'll track this guy down."

He told them that it was a complete win-win. The hotel's liability in the civil suit would go way down if he could show that the victim had not been attacked by a hotel employee. "What could be better?" he said. "Think how good you'll look if we actually catch the guy responsible. You'd be solving a horrible crime!"

They seemed distinctly unmoved.

"Look at how cool this guy is," he told them, replaying the video. "He just raped and beat a woman to death, or thinks he has, and it's not like he's all nervous and jittery. He's cool as a clam! Tell me the kind of person who could do such a thing and be this nonchalant. This ain't the only time he's done this."

A discussion ensued. There were some in the room who wanted to find the rapist, but the decision was primarily a business calculation. It was about weighing the detective's fee against a chance to limit their exposure. Brennan didn't care what their reasons were; he just wanted to keep going. Old instincts had been aroused. He had never even met Inna, but with her attacker in his sights, he wanted him badly. Here was a guy walking around somewhere almost a year later, certain that he had gotten away with his crime. Brennan wanted what all detectives want: the *gotcha!* He wanted to see the look on the guy's face.

It was close, but in the end the hotel suits decided to let him keep working. Having overcome their skepticism so narrowly, Brennan was even more determined to prove he was right.

The hotel's records were useless. There were too many rooms and there was too much turnover to scrutinize every guest. Even if the hotel staff remembered a three-hundred-pound black man with glasses, which they did not, there was no way to tell whether he was a registered hotel guest or a visitor, or if he was sharing someone else's room. Even in cases where the front desk workers photocopied a guest's driver's license, which they did not do faithfully, the image came up so muddy that there was no way to make out the face.

So he went back to the video. Now that he knew whom he was looking for, Brennan scrutinized every appearance of his suspect in the days before the crime, at the elevator, in the lobby, at the hotel restaurant, at the front door. In one of the video snippets at the elevator, the suspect is seen walking with a fit black man wearing a white T-shirt with the word "Mercury" on the front, which meant nothing to Brennan. His first thoughts were the car company or the planet or the element. There was nothing there he could work with. The manner of both men on the snippet suggested that they knew each other. They walked past the elevator and turned to their right, in the direction of the hotel's restaurant. So Brennan hunted for video from the restaurant's surveillance camera, and sure enough, it captured the two entering. As Brennan reviewed more video, he saw the big black man with the other man often, so he suspected that the two had been in town together. The man in the T-shirt had an ID tag on a string around his neck, but it was too small to read it on the screen. Brennan called NASA to see whether they had a way to enhance the picture. He described the camera and was told that it couldn't be done.

Again, back to the video. In the restaurant footage, the man in the T-shirt is momentarily seen from behind, revealing another word on the back of the T-shirt. The best view comes in a split second as he sidesteps around someone leaving, giving the camera a better angle. Brennan could see the letter *V* at the beginning of the word, and *O* at the end. He could make out a vague pattern of script in the middle, but could not be sure of the exact letters. It was like looking at an eye chart when you need stronger glasses; you take a guess. It looked to him as if the word was "Verado." It meant nothing to him, but that was his hunch. So he Googled it and found that "Verado" was the name of a new outboard engine manufactured by Mercury Marine, the boat-engine manufacturer.

There had been a big boat show in Miami in February, when the incident had happened. Perhaps the man in the white T-shirt had been working at the show for Mercury Marine, and if he had, maybe his big friend had too.

Mercury Marine is a subsidiary of the Brunswick Corporation, which also manufactures billiards and bowling equipment and other recreational products. Brennan called Brunswick's head of security, Alan Sperling, and explained what he was trying to do. His first thought was that the company might have put its boat show employees up at the Airport Regency. If it had, he might be able to identify and locate the man in the picture through the company. Sperling checked; no, Mercury's employees had stayed at a different hotel. Brennan racked his brain. Had any of the crews who set up the company's booth stayed at the Regency? Again, the answer was no.

"Well, who got those shirts?" Brennan asked.

Sperling checked and called back two weeks later. He said the only place the shirts had been given away was at the boat show's food court. The company in charge of food for the show was called Centerplate, which handles concessions for large sporting events and conventions. It was a big company with employees spread across the nation. Brennan called the head of human resources for Centerplate, who told him that the company had put up some of its people at the Regency, but that it had hired more than two hundred for the boat show, from all over.

"Somebody has to remember a big black guy, three hundred pounds at least—in glasses," said the detective.

A week later, the man from Centerplate called back. Some of the company's workers did remember a big black man with glasses, but no one knew his name. Someone did seem to recall, he said, that the company had initially hired the man to work at Zephyr Field, home of the New Orleans Zephyrs, the minor league baseball team in Metairie, Louisiana, a sprawling suburb. This was a solid lead, but there was a problem with it: Hurricane Katrina had devastated the city just months earlier, and the residents of Metairie had been evacuated. It was a community scattered to the winds.

Brennan was stubborn. He was now months into this effort to identify and find the man responsible for raping and beating a woman he had never met. There was no way that what he was being paid for the job was worth the hours he was putting in. Nobody else cared as much as he did. What the hotel's insurers really wanted, Brennan knew, was for him to tell them that Budnytska was a hooker and that she had been beaten by one of her johns, which would go a long way toward freeing them from any liability. But this wasn't true, and he had told them at the outset that the truth was all they would get from him. Detective Foote of the Miami-Dade police was openly skeptical. He had given Brennan all the information he had. He had more pressing cases with real leads and real prospects.

But Brennan had a picture in his head. He could see this big man with glasses coolly going about his business day to day—smug, chatting up the women, no doubt looking for his next victim, comfortable, certain that his crimes left no trail.

Katrina created a problem with the New Orleans lead, but on the plus side, Brennan had a buddy on the police force there, a Captain Ernest Demma. Some years earlier, on a vacation to the French Quarter with his kids, Brennan had risked his hide helping Demma subdue a prisoner who had violently turned on him.

"The guy had broken away from me," Demma recalled, "and out of nowhere comes this guy in a black jacket flying down the sidewalk, who runs him down, tackles him, and held the guy until my men could subdue him. He was fantastic." It was the kind of gesture a cop never forgets. Demma dubbed Brennan "Batman." New Orleans may have been down for the count, but when Batman called, Demma was up for anything.

The captain sent one of his sergeants out to Zephyr Field, where the club was working overtime to get its storm-ravaged facility ready to open the 2006 season. Demma called Brennan back: "The good news is, I know who this guy is."

"What's the bad news?"

"His name is Mike Jones, there's probably only a million of them, and he doesn't work there anymore, and nobody knows where he went."

Still, a name! Brennan thanked Demma and went back to
the Regency database, and sure enough, he found that there
had indeed been a guest named Mike Jones staying at the hotel
when the attack occurred. He had checked in on February 14,
seven days before the rape and assault, and he had checked out
on February 22, one day after he was seen rolling his suitcase
out to the car. The full name on his Visa card was Michael Lee
Jones. The card had been canceled, and the address was for a
Virginia residence Jones had vacated years earlier. He had left no
forwarding address. Brennan lacked the authority to subpoena
further information from the credit card company, and the evidence he had was still too slight to get the Miami-Dade police
involved. The phone number Jones had left with registration was
a number for Centerplate.

But the trail was warm again. Brennan knew that Jones no
longer worked for Centerplate, and the people there didn't know
where he was, but the detective thought he knew certain things
about his prey. Judging by the nonchalance he showed hauling
a young woman's body out of the hotel stuffed in a suitcase,
Brennan suspected that this was a practiced routine. The Centerplate job had kept him moving from city to city, all expenses
paid, a perfect setup for a serial rapist with a method that was
tried and true. If Jones was his man, then he wouldn't give up
an arrangement like that. If he wasn't employed by Centerplate
anymore, where would somebody with his work experience go
next? Who was facilitating his predation now? Brennan got some
names from Centerplate and went online to compile a list of the
food-service company's top twenty to twenty-five competitors.

He started working his way down the list, calling human
resources for each of the competing firms, and one by one he

struck out. As it happened, one company on the list, Ovations, had its headquarters in the Tampa area, and Brennan was planning a trip up in that direction anyway, so he decided to drop in. As any investigator will tell you, an interview in person is always better than an interview on the phone. Brennan stopped by and, as he can do, talked his way into the office of the company's chief operating officer. He explained his manhunt, and asked whether Ovations employed a three-hundred-plus-pound black man with glasses named Michael Lee Jones.

The executive didn't even check a database. He told Brennan, who was not a law-enforcement official, that if he wanted that information he would have to return with a subpoena. All the other companies had checked a database and just told Brennan no. He knew he had finally asked in the right place.

"Why would you want someone working for you who is a rapist?" he asked. He was told there were privacy issues involved.

"Get a subpoena," the executive suggested.

So Brennan got a fax number for Ovations and called Detective Foote at Miami-Dade; before long a subpoena spat from the fax machine. It turned out that Ovations had an employee named Michael Lee Jones who fit the description. He was now working in Frederick, Maryland.

Michael Lee Jones was standing behind a barbeque counter at Harry Grove Stadium, home of the minor-league Frederick Keys, when Detective Foote and one of his partners showed up. It was an early-spring evening in the Appalachian foothills, and Foote the Floridian was so cold his teeth were chattering beneath his mustache.

When Brennan had called him with the information about Jones, Foote was impressed by the private detective's tenacity, but still skeptical. This whole effort more or less defined the term "long shot," but the name and location of a potential suspect was without question the first real lead since the case had landed on his desk. It had to be checked out. The department had a requirement that detectives traveling out of town to confront suspected criminals go as a team, so Foote had waited until another detective had to make such a trip to the suburbs of Washington, DC. He got the detective to agree to take him along as partner. Together they then made the hour-and-a-half drive from DC to Frederick to visit Jones in person.

Foote had called Jones earlier that day to see whether he would be available. The detective kept it vague. He just said he was investigating an incident in Miami that had happened during the boat show, and he confirmed that Jones had been working there. On the phone, Jones was polite and forthcoming. He said he'd been in Miami at that time and that he would be available to meet with Foote, and gave him directions to the ballpark.

Jones was a massive man. Tall, wide, and powerful, with long arms and big hands and a great round belly. His size was intimidating, but his manner was exceedingly soft-spoken and gentle, even passive. He wore clear-rimmed glasses and spoke in a friendly way. Jones was in charge of the operation at the food counter and appeared to be respected and well liked by his busy employees. He was wearing an apron. He steered Foote and the other detective away from the booth to a picnic area just outside the stadium.

As Foote recalled it later, he asked Jones about meeting women in Miami, and Jones said he had "hooked up" once. The detective asked him to describe her. "I only have sex with white women," Jones said.

Foote asked if he had had sex with anyone at the Airport Regency, and Jones said no. He said that the woman he'd had sex with in Miami had been working at the boat show, and that they had hooked up elsewhere.

"Any blonde women?" Foote asked.

"No."

"Foreign accent?"

Jones said the woman he'd had sex with in Miami had been German.

Foote was not making Jones as a suspect. The big man acted convincingly, like someone with nothing to hide. The detective was freezing in the evening air. Foote preferred coming right to the point anyway; he was not given to artful interrogation. Besides, he felt more and more as if the trip had been a waste of time. So he just asked what he wanted to know.

"Look, I've got a girl who was raped that week. Did you have anything to do with it?"

"No, of course not!" said Jones, appropriately shocked by the question. "No way."

"You didn't beat the shit out of this girl and leave her for dead in a field down there?"

"Oh, no. No."

"Are you willing to give me a DNA specimen?" Foote asked.

Jones promptly said he would, further convincing the detective that this was not the guy. Do the guilty volunteer conclusive evidence? He only knew of one prior case where one did—"and that guy was a complete idiot," he said. Jones did not strike him as an idiot. He retrieved his kit from the car and ran a cotton inside of Jones's mouth. Convinced Brennan had enlisted him in a classic wild goose chase, Foote carried the specimen back to Miami, submitted it for lab analysis, and called Brennan.

"I'm telling you, Ken, this ain't the guy," he said.

"No, man, he's definitely the fucking guy," said Brennan, who flew up to Frederick himself, traveling with his son, and spent time over a three-day period talking to Jones, who continued to deny everything.

Months after he returned, the DNA results came back. Brennan got a call from Foote.

"You ain't going to believe this," said Foote.

"What?"

"You were right."

Jones's DNA was a match.

Brennan flew up to Frederick in October to meet Foote, who arrested the big man. It had been eleven months since he took the case. Foote formally charged Jones with a variety of felonies that encompassed the acts of raping, kidnapping, and severely beating Inna Budnytska. The accused sat forlornly in a chair that looked tiny under his bulk, in an austere Frederick Police Department interrogation room, great rolls of fat falling on his lap under an enormous Baltimore Ravens T-shirt. He repeatedly denied everything in a surprisingly soft voice peculiar for such a big man, gesturing broadly with both hands, protesting but never growing angry, and insisting that he would never, ever, under any circumstances, do such a thing to a woman. He said that he "never had any problems" paying women for sex and that he "did not get a kick" out of hurting women. He did admit, once the DNA test irrevocably linked him to Budnytska, that he had had sex with her, but insisted that she was a "hooker," that he had paid her a hundred dollars, and that when he left her she was in fine shape, although very drunk. They showed him pictures of her battered face taken the day she was found.

"I did not hurt that girl," Jones said, pushing the photos away, his voice rising to a whine. "I'm not violent. . . . I never hit a fucking woman in my whole fucking life! I'm not going to hurt her."

Brennan asked him why a man would roll his suitcase out to the parking lot and stash it in his car at five in the morning, two days before he checked out of the hotel.

"I couldn't remember if we were leaving that day or the next day. I wasn't sure. . . . For some reason, I thought, 'Fuck it, it's time to go.'"

Brennan was able to trip Jones up with only one small thing. Jones said that his suitcase had only his clothes, shoes, and a video game in it, but when the detective noted the extra tug Jones had needed to get it off the elevator, Jones suddenly remembered that he had had a number of large books in it as well. He said he was an avid reader.

When Brennan asked him to name some of the books he had read, Jones could not. He could not name a single title.

But Jones was unfailingly compliant, and his manner worked for him. Even with the DNA, the case against him was weak. He had ample reason for not having volunteered initially that he had paid a woman for sex—he had a prior arrest for soliciting a prostitute—so that wouldn't count against him, and if he'd had consensual sex with Budnytska, as he said, it would account for the DNA. The fact that Jones had willingly provided the sample spoke in his favor. In court, it would come down to his word against Inna's, and she was a terrible witness. She had picked

Jones out of a photo lineup, but given how foggy her memory of the night was, and the fact that she had seen Jones before, unlike the other faces she was shown, it was hardly convincing evidence of his guilt. Her initial accounts of the crime were so much at odds with Brennan's findings that even Foote found himself wondering who was telling the truth.

Miami prosecutors ended up settling with Jones, who, after being returned to Miami, pleaded guilty to sexual assault in return for having all of the more severe charges against him dropped. He was sentenced to two years in prison, an outcome that Brennan would have found very disappointing if that had been the end of the story. It was not.

Brennan never doubted that Jones was a rapist, and given what he had observed, first on the surveillance video and then after meeting him in person, he was convinced that sexual assault was Jones's pastime.

"This ain't a one-fucking-time deal," Brennan told Foote. "I'm telling you, this is this guy's thing. He's got a job that sends him all over the country. Watch him on that video. He's slick. Nonchalant. He's too cool, too calm. You'll see it when you put his DNA into the system."

The "system" is the Combined DNA Index System (CODIS). The FBI administered database now has well over eight million DNA offender profiles. Local, state, and federal law enforcement officials routinely enter DNA samples recovered from convicts and from the scenes and victims of unsolved crimes, and over the years the system has electronically matched more than a hundred thousand of them, often reaching across surprising

THE CASE OF THE VANISHING BLONDE 115

distances in place and time. It means that if a DNA sample exists, a case can never be classified as entirely "cold."

Michael Lee Jones had left a trail. The Miami-Dade police entered Jones's DNA into CODIS in late 2006, and several months later, which is how long it takes the FBI to double-check matches the system finds electronically, three new hits came up.

Detective Terry Thrumston of the Colorado Springs Police Department's sex-crimes unit had a rape and assault case that had been bugging her for more than a year. The victim was a blonde-haired, blue-eyed woman who had been picked up early in the morning on December 1, 2005, by a stranger—a very large black man with glasses, who had offered her a ride and then talked his way into her apartment and raped her, holding his hand tightly over her mouth. Thrumston had no leads, and the case had sat for two years, until DNA collected from the victim matched with that of Michael Lee Jones.

There were two victims in New Orleans. One of them, also a blonde, had been partying in the French Quarter a little too hard, by her own admission, and very early on the morning of May 5, 2003, she had gone looking for a cab back to her hotel, when a very large black man with glasses had pulled his car over to the curb and offered her a ride. As she later testified, he drove her to a weedy lot and raped her. He pressed his large hand powerfully over her face as he attacked her, and she testified that she had bit into his palm so hard that she had bits of his skin in her teeth afterward. When he was finished, he drove off, leaving her on the lot. She reported the rape to the New Orleans police, who filed her account and took DNA samples from the rapist's semen. The case had sat until CODIS matched the specimen with Michael Lee Jones. The other New Orleans victim told a similar tale, but failed to pick Jones's face out of a photo lineup.

Jones, it turns out, had been in both Colorado Springs and New Orleans on the dates in question. So in 2008, as his two-year Florida sentence drew to a close, he was flown out to Colorado Springs to stand trial. It was a novel prosecution, because the Colorado woman had died in the interim of causes unrelated to the crime. As a result, Deputy District Attorney Brien Cecil had no victim to put on the stand. Instead, he fashioned a case out of two of the other rapes, calling as witnesses Budnytska and one of the New Orleans victims, both of whom supplemented the DNA evidence by pointing out Jones as their attacker in the courtroom. Cecil argued that their cases showed a "common plan, scheme, or design" that was as much Jones's signature as his trail of semen.

The New Orleans victim proved to be a very effective witness. Her memory was clear and her statements emphatic, the outrage still evident six years later, along with her chagrin at the poor judgment she had displayed that night. Inna, on the other hand, was every bit as bad on the stand as the Miami prosecutors had feared. One of Jones's lawyers made much of the different stories she had told police. Her struggles with English further confused matters.

Jones pleaded not guilty to all charges in the Colorado case. He argued through his lawyers (he did not testify) that the sex had been consensual, and that the woman claiming rape had been a prostitute. But where jurors in Colorado might have been able to accept two prostitutes in different states at different times unaccountably filing rape charges after turning a trick, and in both cases immediately describing their attacker as a huge black man with glasses, they clearly choked on a third. There was no evidence that any of the victims were prostitutes. And then, of course, there was the DNA.

Michael Lee Jones is serving what amounts to a life sentence at the Fremont Correctional Facility in Colorado. He received a term of twenty-four years to life for one count of sexual assault and twelve years to life for the second count, of felonious sexual contact. He is thirty-eight years old and will not be eligible for his first parole hearing until 2032. The state estimates his term will last until he dies.

Budnytska won a $300,000 settlement from the hotel and the hotel's security company.

Ken Brennan is back doing his private detective work in Miami. He is enormously proud of the efforts that have locked Jones away. "The cases they got him on, they're just the tip of the iceberg," he predicted. "Once other jurisdictions start checking their DNA files on cases when this guy was at large, I guarantee you they will find more."

So far his hunches have been pretty good.

. . . A Million Years Ago

Vanity Fair, July 2012

Los Angeles Police Department detective Stephanie Lazarus has a very expressive, elastic face. At fifty-one she looks at least ten years younger. Her straight brown hair is shoulder-length, with bangs that fall at an angle to either side of her forehead, and her manner is outgoing and friendly. She is pretty, even as middle age has begun to tug at her face. She smiles and laughs easily and has a wide range of comical facial expressions but she is mercurial—she has a quick, harsh temper. She can also turn on a hard, weathered expression, a look that means business and that is useful for someone who has spent the last quarter century as a cop.

On the morning of June 5, 2009, Lazarus reported for work at the Parker Center, the LAPD administration building downtown, where she was surrounded by many of her longtime colleagues and friends. She was a respected, well-known figure in the department. No, more than that. In this close-knit world, she was in her own way legendary. She had worked her way up from a patrol car to heading the art-theft division, a fascinating job that was about more than crime fighting. It had a public-relations aspect to it, in that stolen art tends to be stolen from the homes and galleries of some of LA's most notable citizens. It was a coveted job in the LAPD. There was no getting bogged down with a heavy caseload, no being under the thumb of a supervisor. The unit had only two detectives; they met fascinating people, and there was a great deal of freedom in choosing which cases to pursue. And there was no doubt Lazarus deserved it. In all of her years in the department, she had never had a disciplinary hearing. Not one. This was unheard of, and it had made Lazarus famous. She had covered most of the desired positions in the LAPD, in units such as DARE (Drug Abuse Resistance Education), Homicide, and Internal Affairs. She was widely known in the department and well liked, despite her gloss of perfection. She could be chipper and fun. She had married a fellow detective, and together they had adopted a child. She had survived a bout with cancer. Lazarus had started up the department's childcare program, had initiated a child-safety/ ID program. She was one of those people whom it was, simply, a privilege to know.

When Detective Dan Jaramillo asked Lazarus for help that morning, she was predictably eager to oblige. He told her that they had arrested someone who had information about an art theft and asked her if she would go downstairs with him to the building's basement jail facility to interrogate the suspect. They walked downstairs together, chatting amiably. Lazarus was led into a small interrogation room with pale blue walls and soundproof tiles from about waist level to the ceiling. Here Jaramillo introduced her to his partner, Greg Stearns.

They asked Lazarus to take a seat in the chair ordinarily given to the interrogatee. This clearly felt odd to her. She had a concerned, querulous look on her face as she sat down, but she was still very collegial. Lazarus was here to help.

"I did not want to bring this up in your squad room," said Jaramillo, in a friendly, confidential way.

"You're going to bring someone in, right?" she asked.

Jaramillo deflected the question. He repeated what he had started to say and then went on: "People are always listening [up there], wondering what everybody else is doing . . ."

He made it clear, without alarming her, that the art-theft story had been a ruse. This was about something else, something that concerned her. The detectives had her full attention.

"We've been assigned a case," said Jaramillo. "And there are some notes as far as your name being mentioned."

"Oh," said Lazarus. The look on her face was theatrically bewildered. "OK," she said, skeptically.

"Do you know John Ruetten?"

Jaramillo had pronounced it wrong, "*Root*-en," and after a long moment she corrected him. "Do you mean John *Rutt*-en?"

"Yes," said the detective.

"Yeah, I went to school with him. . . . Let's see. I went to UCLA. Nineteen seventy-eight I started, and, you know, I met him at school, in the dorms."

"Were you guys friends? Close friends?"

"Yeah. We were very close friends. I mean, what's this all about?"

Lazarus sat forward in her chair. Challenging.

"It's a case we're working on that involves John, and in . . . some of the things we reviewed, there's notes and stuff that he knew you."

"Oh, yeah. We were friends. We lived in the dorms for two years."

"You guys lived in the same dorm?"

"Yeah. . . . Dykstra."

"OK," said Jaramillo. "Were you guys just friends, or anything else?"

"Yeah. We were good friends."

"Was there any kind of relationship or anything that developed between you guys?"

"Yeah," said Lazarus, mildly put out. Very mildly. This was personal, but she was in her fraternal mode, which ran deep with her. She seemed determined to be helpful. "I mean, we dated," she said. "You know. . . " And then, leaning forward, she asked confidentially, cop to cop, "I mean, what's this all about?" *Clue me in here, would you guys?*

"Well, it's relating to his wife."

"O-kaay," she said, drawing the word out. *Why are you asking me such a bizarre question, out of the blue?*

"Did you know her?"

"Not really. I mean, I knew that he got married years ago."

"Did you ever meet her?"

"God, I don't know."

"Did you know who she was or anything?"

"Well, let me think." She leaned back in her chair and looked off for a moment, closing her eyes. Her expression also conveyed annoyed surprise, but Jaramillo was speaking softly and politely, and she was on board. "God, it's been a long time ago," she said, twisting her face at last in a bewildered grimace, as if the question had been preposterous but she was still willing to comply.

"I may have met her. . . . *Jeez*," she said, raising her hands in exasperation. "You know."

John Ruetten was crazy about Sherri Rasmussen. They met in the summer of 1984, John a talkative, charming young man with a thick mop of dark hair, as handsome as a male model, and Sherri a tall Scandinavian beauty with light brown hair, a broad face with high cheekbones, and wide-set eyes under dark, arching eyebrows. Both were lean and athletic, runners, and both were on a fast track. He was a recent graduate of UCLA, and she was, just two years older at twenty-seven, already the director of nursing at the Glendale Adventist Medical Center.

Sherri was hot stuff. She had entered Loma Linda University at age sixteen and now lectured internationally on critical-care nursing. She was beautiful, and she was considered brilliant. She was also confident and directed. She was the kind of person John wanted to be, or, rather, a personification of how he saw himself in his best moments. And she fell just as hard for him. Their connection was immediate and untroubled. It was as though everything else in their lives just fell away when they met, old relationships, future plans. They met, and they were together. Just like that. Over Memorial Day weekend in 1985, they drove down to San Diego, where John's parents lived and where Sherri's kept a boat, and announced their engagement. John put down his life savings on a silver BMW that same weekend and gave it to Sherri as a present— he drove a red Mazda RX-7, so now they both had cars that announced jaunty horizons. They were married in November 1985. Months earlier, John had moved into Sherri's Van Nuys condominium, up in the San Fernando Valley region of LA, against the dramatic backdrop of the Transverse mountains.

It had been a busy holiday season after the wedding, with happy visits to both sets of parents, and by Monday, February 24, of the following year, John and Sherri were settling into the comfortable rhythm of married life. John had started a job with an engineering company. When he left their Van Nuys condominium for work that day, Sherri was still in bed. Ordinarily, she left for work first, but they had gone out to a movie Sunday night and gotten home late, and she was not eager to be off. She was supposed to supervise a human resources class for some of her nursing charges that morning, and she didn't feel like doing it. It was mandated by the hospital, but Sherri was less than sold on its value. She told John she was thinking about just calling in sick and staying home that day. He encouraged her to just go in and get the class over with. She was still undecided and under the covers when he walked out the front door at about 7:20.

On his way to work, John dropped off some laundry and was at his desk shortly before eight. He thought about calling Sherri—they normally talked often during the day—but he didn't want to disturb her if she had decided to sleep in. He tried mid-morning, and when there was no answer assumed she had taken his advice and decided to teach the class after all. He tried her office, but her secretary said she hadn't seen her yet. On Mondays when she taught the class, the secretary said, she sometimes didn't come by her office at all. John tried to reach her at home three or four more times but did not get an answer.

It was odd that the answering machine had not been turned on, but Sherri sometimes forgot. He was not especially concerned.

On his way home early that evening John ran some errands, stopping by the dry cleaner to pick up the freshly laundered clothes, and a UPS store, and when he pulled up to the garage behind the condo, was surprised to see the door drawn up. The Balboa Townhomes consisted of white three-story mock-Tudor buildings with garage entrances on the ground floor in the back alley. Just above the garage was a small balcony before two sliding glass doors. John and Sherri sometimes sat out there side by side in deck chairs. On either side of the garage door were two small trees staked in planters. Their ten-speed bikes and a tool bench were against the back wall. There was no space for clutter; the garage was just wide enough for their two cars. Sherri's BMW was gone, and there were shards of broken glass on the pavement at the entrance. John's first thought was that this must be glass from one of her car windows. She must have run into while something pulling out. Weeks earlier, she had clipped the door and broken the aerial on her car. He thought, "Uh-oh, what did she do now?" That might also explain why she had not closed the garage door. If she were flustered, she might have just driven off. He lifted the plastic bag of dry cleaning out of the car and headed up the garage stairs to the living room. It wasn't until he saw that the inner door to their living room was ajar that he grew alarmed.

Sherri was dead on the floor of the living room. She lay on her back on the brown rug, her face swollen, battered, and bloody. She was barefoot, still in her red bathrobe. At first he thought that she was, maybe, asleep, but when he saw her face he knew, as he would tell a detective later, "we were in trouble."

Those who die violently leave life in mid-stride, often with a look of terminal surprise on their face, frozen. Sherri's robe was thrown open, her arms were raised and bent, and one long, slender leg was slightly raised and bent at the knee. She looked fixed in the act of trying to get up. John touched her leg, and it was stiff. Her skin was cold. He put his fingers to her wrist to feel for a pulse. There was none.

He was struck—and "struck" is the right word—by the sheer impossibility of what he saw. You heard about such things, of course. There would be 831 homicides in Los Angeles that year. But hearing about them never made the prospect of such a thing possible in your own life. John walked around the living room wordlessly, staring at his wife's unnaturally stiff body, trying to accept that she was *not going to get up.* More than grief or wonder or confusion, one feels stunned by the sudden appearance of the impossible, as if one has collided hard with an invisible wall. Here was Sherri, so alive to him in every way, still so vividly and shockingly present and yet irremediably, utterly gone. Her face was covered with dried blood, the right eyelid bluish and puffy and closed. Her left eye was open, staring up, and her mouth was open in a final gasp. She had been dead for hours. Just below the rim of her delicate, form-fitting pink camisole, right in the center of her chest, was a black bullet hole.

John phoned 911.

"I think my wife is dead," he said.

He paced the living room and stared down at her with disbelief. Then he took a blanket and covered her. He could not stand being in the room with her body, with the reality of her death, but he also felt he could not leave. He paced some more, walked back down to the garage, and then came back up to the living room, standing over her, bobbing slowly back and forth, too numb to cry or even feel, waiting for the police to arrive and make this nightmare official.

"You know," Lazarus had said with exasperation. Her tone and expression made it clear that being asked about the wife of a former boyfriend was not only none of their business but also totally out of line. But Jaramillo pressed on, speaking in the same soft, insistent voice. He was not going to fully explain himself, at least not yet.

"Let me ask you," he said. "You said you dated John. How long did you guys date?"

This was finally too much for Lazarus.

"I mean, what? Is this *something*?" she said, looking mystified. "I mean, you said this was going to be about art, and now you change our . . . I mean?"

She was not going forward without some kind of explanation. So Jaramillo's partner, Greg Stearns, explained.

"Stephanie, here's the situation," Greg Stearns said. "Basically, we knew when we saw in this chrono that maybe there was some relationship there. That's what the chrono seems to indicate, and we didn't want to come up to you at your desk and ask those kind of questions or do anything . . ."

As Stearns explained, Lazarus listened with a pained smile on her face, nodding at intervals briskly and mechanically, saying "OK" nervously to indicate that she understood.

She was experienced enough with this kind of work to realize by now that she was being played. She might have just stood up and walked out . . . but how would that look? Whatever options occurred to her, she remained friendly, if annoyed.

You could see she wanted to know what was going on, which was reason enough to stay. How much did these detectives have? Were they just poking around in the old files, just getting started, chasing down every angle, or did they have something? It was prudent to assume they had more than they were letting on.

"I mean, God, it's been a million years ago," she said.

But she was willing to proceed. She described her relationship with John in college, all the while shaking her head with bewilderment. They had hung around together with a group of friends. "We did things. I played sports in college. He played basketball. His brother played basketball. It didn't work out. I don't know what to tell you . . ." John had been just one of a circle of friends from those dorm years at UCLA with whom she had stayed in touch. Nothing special. They had gone to Hawaii together at some point, but had not spoken in years. "I couldn't even tell you the last time I talked to him. It was kind of a weird relationship," she said. "We dated. I can't say that he was my boyfriend. I don't know if he would have considered me his girlfriend. We just dated."

"Had you met his wife?" asked Jaramillo.

"I may have."

"Do you remember her name or anything?"

"Ummm . . ." she said, straining to recall something insignificant from very long ago.

"Or what she did for a living, or where she worked, or anything about her?"

"Well, I think she was a nurse. I can't even remember how he said he met her. It's been so long ago."

"Did you go to their wedding?"

"No. I didn't go to their wedding. No. I . . . I can't even tell you what year they got married. It's been a million years ago. . . . Again, I don't understand why you are talking about some guy I dated a million years ago."

They talked more about the dating scene at UCLA. Asked if she had ever associated with Ruetten after he married, Lazarus had a curious answer. "I don't *think* so," she said. She asked again why they were questioning her about this.

"Do you know what happened to his wife?"

"Yeah. I know she got killed."

"What did you hear about that?"

"I saw a poster at work. I'm sure I spoke to him about it. Um, I think I spoke to another friend of his about it . . ."

The crime scene was meticulously documented in 1986. It looked as if there had been a fight.

One of the living room's tall stereo speakers was knocked over and lying beside Sherri on the rug, its top flush against her head. The wires had been removed from it. A gray ceramic vase with a heavy base lay shattered on the floor. The top two shelves of the wooden display cabinet had been knocked askew, and an amplifier and receiver dangled forward on top of the television. A decorative display of dried plants had been knocked off the coffee table and was on the floor at the foot of the couch. The drawer of a side table had been pulled out completely, its contents strewn across the rug. At the base of the stairs leading up from the living room to the second floor, a VCR and a CD player had been stacked neatly, as if assembled for carrying out but then left behind. There was a single bloody smudge on top of the CD player. There were smears of blood on the east wall of the condo and another smear on the front door. On the floor just inside the front door were two intertwined cords; one was apparently the wire from the fallen speaker. Upstairs, one of the two glass sliding doors to the back balcony was shattered. This was the glass John had seen on the pavement outside the garage. There was no sign of forced entry, and other than the disarray and the objects left on the living-room floor, there was no sign of ransacking anywhere else in the house.

Homicide detective Lyle Mayer discovered that a pink and pale green quilted blanket on the living-room chair had a bullet hole in it, with associated powder burns. He recognized two holes of what turned out to be three holes in Sherri's chest as contact wounds—in other words, after the first shot, a gun had been placed against her chest and fired point blank, twice. It appeared that the killer had used the blanket to muffle the sound. This had been an execution.

Two bullets were recovered from Sherri's body, both .38 caliber; one of the bullets must have passed completely through her. Any of these three shots alone would have been rapidly fatal. Somebody had wanted to make sure she was dead. In addition to the wounds on her face—it was likely she had been struck over her right eye with the vase—there was a bite mark on her inner left forearm. It would be swabbed for saliva samples, and a cast would be taken for a possible tooth comparison. There were also marks on Sherri's wrists, which suggested that at some point they had been bound.

John told police about his day, retracing his steps for them. Over the next few weeks, police investigators under Mayer's supervision interviewed neighbors, family members, and friends, but turned up no suspects. The silver BMW was found a week later parked on a street in Van Nuys, unlocked, keys in the ignition. Investigators found several fingerprints in it, a spot of blood, and a strand of brown hair. Research and neighborhood interviews revealed that two Latino men had been breaking into houses in the area, and that in one case they had assaulted a woman. The opinion Mayer formed that first day would not change.

"I believe your house was burglarized today, sometime before ten a.m.," he told a distraught John that night, just hours after the shocked husband had called 911. After more than an hour of detailed questioning, the detective assured John that he, Mayer, did not suspect him of any involvement. "I believe they got in your front door," he said. "I don't think it was locked. . . . Once those persons or that person or whoever was inside, I believe they were trying to steal your stereo and probably some other items."

"Why would they do anything to her?" asked John, crying. "Why wouldn't they just run?"

"I don't know, John," said Mayer. "John, things happen, OK? Here's what I think happened. I think Sherri came down the stairs. And I think she surprised them. And she was hurt, OK? . . . She was shot."

Mayer said Sherri's body was then dragged down to the living room. After delivering this analysis, he asked John, almost as an afterthought, whether he and Sherri had been having any problems.

"We were having the *best time,*" John said, sobbing. "We just got married." It was hard not to be moved by his grief.

"No financial problems? She's not having problems with an ex-boyfriend; or you with an ex-girlfriend?"

"No," said John.

The interrogation of Stephanie Lazarus was a dance. For the detectives, the idea was to delay turning the conversation into a confrontation for as long as possible. Lazarus had her own moves. She kept turning the discussion to other matters, working to keep things friendly and collegial; laughing and referring to mutual acquaintances; mugging wonder, surprise, confusion, irritation; gesturing broadly with her hands; working to keep the discussion at the level of cop talk and going on about The Job, even as Jaramillo and Stearns zeroed in on darker turf. She reviewed her dating history, ticking off the men she had dated in her youth before she had met her husband, and making sure that John Ruetten was seen as a blip, just one in a fairly large group, and that their relationship was, as she said over and over again, "a million years ago." How could they expect her to remember this stuff?

"When you heard about John's wife being killed, what was your reaction?" asked Jaramillo.

"I obviously called the family. I called some of his friends that I knew. Obviously, it's shocking to hear. . . . I can't say if I initially spoke to him or not. I honestly don't remember. I may have said to somebody, 'Hey, have him call me if he wants to talk.' And then he may have done that."

"Do you know what the circumstances were regarding her death?"

"Ummm. Jeez. Let me think back. Umm. Jeez." Here she screwed up her face as if struggling to recall an utterly insignificant detail. "I don't know if it was a burglary or something, it's been so many years. I can faintly think that I may have seen a flyer. It may have had her picture on it. That's what I see. If somebody called me, I may not have known what her last name was. I may have. Maybe if you told me, I would remember it."

"Do you know the first name?"

"Shelly. Sherri? Something. Like I said, it's been so many years."

"As far as you can remember, do you remember ever talking to her?"

"As I said earlier, I may have, you know. I may have talked to her."

"You mentioned a hospital maybe—you may have talked to her at a hospital," said Stearns.

Suddenly, Lazarus's memory began to thaw.

"Yeah. I may have met her," she said, rolling her eyes. "I'm thinking, now that you guys are bringing up all these old memories. You know. I mean, *jeez*," she said, shaking her head and sighing heavily.

Lazarus was now going to change her story. Not only did she remember John's murdered wife, they had met and talked, probably several times.

She said, "I'm thinking that, because he would date other people and I would date other people, and I think at one point, he may have been dating her. I don't know. Maybe he was married. I don't even remember. And I'm like, 'Why are you calling me if you're dating her, or living with her, or married to her?' I honestly don't remember the time frame. I'm like, 'Come on. Knock it off.' Now I'm thinking, I may have gone to her and said, 'Hey, you know what, if he's dating you, he is bothering me.' I'm thinking we had a conversation about that, one or two, maybe. It could have been three. I don't want to say I had three conversations with her, or whatever."

"At work or at their house?"

"No. I'm thinking, he obviously told me where she worked. I'm thinking it was a hospital somewhere in LA. I could have been . . . again, what year was that? Where was I working?" Another sigh. "I'm trying to think. When did you say they got married?"

"I don't know. I think it was in eighty-five or eighty-six, or something like that," said Jaramillo, disingenuously. He knew exactly when John and Sherri had been married. "We just kind of picked this up. We don't really know a lot about it."

Lazarus counted backward to herself.

"I could have been working in Hollywood, it sounds like, if that's where I was working. And I went and talked to her and just said, 'Hey, you know what, he is dating you, he keeps calling me, why don't you tell him to knock it off or whatever.' Because I probably would have told him to knock it off."

"You would've told John?"

"Oh, yeah. I would have said, 'Hey, you know . . .'"

"But you wanted to tell her too? You wanted them both to know?"

"Yeah, I mean, you are getting calls . . ."

"When you talked to his wife, and said, 'Hey, he keeps calling me, he needs to knock it off,' or what have you, was that civil?"

"Oh, I don't think there was anything," said Lazarus. "The conversation lasted a few moments. I can't even remember. It wasn't like we went out to lunch or anything."

"But there wasn't any arguments or fights, or it didn't get heated?" asked Jaramillo.

"Not that I recall, no. I mean, I would think that would stand out. I would think. Now again, that's not standing out in my mind."

As Nels Rasmussen remembered it years later, the first thing he asked Detective Mayer the day after his daughter was murdered was, "Have you checked out John's ex-girlfriend, the lady cop?"

Nels had answered the phone shortly before one o'clock in the morning at his home in Tucson on Tuesday, February 25, 1986. It was John's father calling with the knee-buckling news.

There was shock, and right away the first sparks of an anger that would never go away. Nels wanted to know why, if his daughter had been killed the day before, he was just being informed of it now. Why hadn't John called him?

Nels is a dentist, a careful, proud, conservative, capable, successful, opinionated man with a rugged tanned face and a shock of snow-white hair. His wife, Loretta, managed his practice. They were enormously proud of their talented daughter and, like many such parents, were less than thrilled about her choice of husband. Nels considered John a pleasant enough fellow but . . . unimpressive. Weak. He had specific reasons for thinking that, reasons apart from the young man's lefty politics. He didn't completely trust John as a man and definitely not as his Sherri's husband. He was not the sort of man he had imagined for her at all. Now those misgivings, which were perfectly normal and which he had sublimated in the face of Sherri's own love for John, had proved prescient in a way far more horrifying than he had ever imagined.

He asked to speak directly to John. He wanted answers. He wanted a detailed accounting of everything that had happened that day, but John's dad, likely apprehending Nels's hostility, refused to put his grieving son on the phone.

Nels sat up the rest of that night, his mind racing, dealing with his shock and pain by noting down everything he knew about the situation. Sherri had confided in him several times in the months since she and John had moved in together. She said this other woman—Nels didn't know her name—had visited their home weeks before their wedding, unannounced. A lady cop. She was dark-haired, athletic, and brazen, and had dropped off a pair of water skis she wanted John to wax. Sherri told her father that she viewed the skis as nothing more than an excuse to intrude, and a provocation. What nerve! She and John had argued afterward, and he had assured her that there was nothing between him and this woman anymore, that they had been dorm pals long before lovers, and that their relationship had never gotten that serious. Still, Sherri did not want him to wax those skis.

According to Nels, John did not back her up, would not stand up to this woman, suggesting instead to Sherri that it would be better to placate her. "I'll just wax them and that will take care of it."

The lady cop had come by again, unannounced, to pick up the skis, Sherri told her father, which John had waxed, despite her objections. That time she asked the woman to leave after John handed over the skis, making it clear that she was unwelcome.

This had not deterred the woman at all. She had shown up again, this time in her LAPD uniform, gun strapped to her waist. She said she was on a break. John had gone to work, and Sherri was still home; usually it was the other way around. Immediately Sherri wondered if this was some kind of routine: fiancée leaves for work and old girlfriend stops by? She didn't want to believe it. She wanted to trust John. The wedding was just weeks away. She cried on the phone while telling her father about it that night, and Sherri did not cry easily. She was used to dealing with life-and-death issues at work. But this lady cop had shaken her. She talked about it more with her father when she and John visited Tucson on her birthday. Nels and Loretta and Sherri and John had gone out to a nightclub to celebrate, and Sherri had waited until she was alone with her father on the dance floor before talking about it; he believed she didn't want to bring it up before John. She said she wished John would just step in and tell this woman to leave them alone, but for some reason he wouldn't do it. This old girlfriend was the only problem she had with him, and all he would do was assure her that the relationship was strictly in the past, that her intrusion was no big deal, that making an issue out of it would just worsen the situation, and that the best thing was just to ignore her until she went away.

Then there was the visit the lady cop had made to Sherri's office at the hospital, the visit Lazarus would admit to twenty-three years later, screwing up her face with the effort to remember something so trifling: "It wasn't like we went out to lunch or anything." Sherri had told her father about this meeting in detail. She said the woman had burst into her office at Glendale, barreling right past the secretary outside her door. This time the lady cop was dressed in tight short-shorts and a form-fitting tube top, an outfit that shouted her sexuality and athleticism. She was shorter than Sherri, but she was fit and strong and moved with a swagger.

Nels brought all of this to Detective Mayer's attention the day after the murder. It was why his immediate question had been, "Have you checked out John's ex-girlfriend, the lady cop?" He would later recall that Mayer dismissed the suggestion out of hand, already wedded to the burglary theory. Nels was told that he had watched too many cop shows on TV.

It is hard to believe Mayer's focus could remain so stubbornly narrow, but in a sense, the detective and the distraught husband had boxed themselves in on the night of the murder. Mayer seems to have seriously considered only two possibilities: one, that John had killed Sherri (most slain women are killed by their intimate partners); and two, that she had been killed by home intruders (the obvious implication of the stereo equipment hastily stacked and left on the floor). Mayer ruled out John as a suspect after talking to him at length. There was no motive, no life insurance policy, no evident trouble in their relationship. You could not help but feel for John. His pain was palpable, unmistakably genuine. The detective was a kind man, and it is clear from their conversation that night that he liked John and came to believe him and trust him. He told John as much at the end of their conversation. So when John dismissed out of hand the notion that an ex-girlfriend might have done this, Mayer was more inclined to believe him than Nels, the angry, grieving father, who seemed to have such irrational suspicion of and dislike for the poor, grieving widower. Speaking with the detective, John disputed Nels's stories. He told Mayer there was no way the confrontations his father-in-law described would have happened without Sherri's telling him about them.

Why would Sherri not have told him the same things she had told her father? She did tell him about Lazarus's hospital visit, but not in a way that made John feel that she had been frightened or even intimidated. What Sherri had conveyed to him was her concern that there might still be something going on between him and Stephanie, which was not true. Perhaps Sherri had simply decided it would be better to deal with the Stephanie problem herself. She was strong and independent and smart. John had moved on. What could the discarded girlfriend do? That was, in effect, what Sherri told Nels the last time they spoke about it.

There may have been another reason Nels wasn't heard. There appears to have been a degree of institutional bias at work that is shocking and perhaps even criminal. The case record suggests that one or more persons, during initial investigation and continuing through the next ten years, were not just disinclined to consider that one of their own had murdered Sherri Rasmussen—they had actively conspired to hide evidence that might have proved it. For one thing, all of the records in the Rasmussen file pertaining to Nels's suspicions about the "lady cop," and even the interview with John the day after the murder, in which he discussed Lazarus with Mayer, are missing. There are audio recordings and notes of every other interview in those first days, which was standard operating procedure, but there are none for the ones in which Lazarus was specifically mentioned. These are conversations remembered by both Nels and John, who were interviewed independently, without knowledge of what the other had said. As we shall see, this suspicious behavior continued in the coming years.

Soon after the murder, Nels was shown sketches of two Latino male suspects, and the burglary theory was explained. There was no way for him to recognize the drawings, and the whole scenario did not make sense to him. He had to wonder about the competence of these detectives. The apartment showed signs of a protracted fight. Mayer estimated that the struggle may have lasted for an hour and a half. How could his daughter have fought off two men for that long? Nels asked. There was the bite mark on her forearm, which had led Mayer's partner, Steve Hooks, to conjecture that the suspect may have been a woman, on the theory that women are biters. But the notion was dismissed. Women don't typically engage in breaking and entering, and fighting men have been known to use their teeth. There was also the bullet wound in the center of Sherri's chest, and the hole and powder burns on the blanket. Mayer told Nels that his daughter had not simply been shot and killed; she had been executed. Why would a burglar do that?

Nels asked if they had checked to see whether the lady cop had been working that day. Had they examined her? Taken pictures of her? If she had been in that fight, there would likely be marks. The answers were no. No one had ever checked up on Lazarus. Mayer or Hooks or someone apparently did talk to her on the phone eventually, and the conversation was considered enough to close that line of inquiry. There is only one brief entry in the case file that mentions her, recorded on November 19, 1987, more than a year and a half after the murder. It reads, "John Ruetten called. Verified Stephanie Lazarus, PO [Police Officer], was former girlfriend." No arrests were ever made in the case. The evidence of Sherri Rasmussen's murder was packed away in commercial storage.

In the interrogation room that June day twenty-three years later, the questioning of Lazarus ground on with Jaramillo and Stearns excavating her memory from "a million years ago."

"And you're saying, when you went to see her, do you remember if it was at her house or at the place she worked at?"

"No, I'm thinking it was probably . . . for some reason I want to say, you know . . . I'm thinking that maybe the hospital was on my way to work in Hollywood. That's maybe sounding familiar."

"Would you have approached her on duty?"

"Oh, no, I'm pretty sure I wouldn't. I'm not saying you haven't done stuff on duty, but I would be working with someone, so I wouldn't. . . . I try to avoid doing stuff on duty."

"Oh, OK. So if it was en route to work, you would more than likely have gone to her work and had this discussion with her?"

"That is sounding familiar. Now that you guys are bringing this stuff up, that sounds familiar. But, again, I mean, you know, what does it have to do with me dating him and her being killed? I don't have anything to do with it."

She had gone from not remembering if she had ever met John's wife, to dimly recalling her name, to acknowledging that they had met on several occasions, including once when she had paid a surprise visit to Sherri's hospital office, woman-to-woman, the ex-girlfriend confronting the new wife. Was that the sort of encounter one forgets?

By now Lazarus would have clearly seen the connection they were making, but she didn't back off. She kept talking, apparently wanting to allow for the possibility that they really did not view her as a suspect. She also apparently did not wish to abandon the possibility that all this was happening only because her name had turned up in the old files. Stearns seemed to want that fiction maintained as well, because he rapidly retreated from the idea that this questioning was anything beyond routine.

"Like I said, we just literally got this the other day, and we're going through it, and you see your name."

"Yeah. Then you saw that I work next door."

"Right, we recognized the name, and we know you work next door to us, and so we are trying to get some background, we're trying to figure this out. I mean, this is from a long time ago." He told her again that the only reason they brought her downstairs to the interview room was to avoid exploring these personal details before her coworkers.

"I appreciate it," she said. "I mean, I appreciate it. This goes way back. I mean, it's very sad, you know, obviously . . ."

Jaramillo had another question. "Let me ask you this: Did the detectives ever reach out to you?"

"No. No one has ever talked to me about him," she said, and then caught herself, screwing up her face again, scratching her head. There would be a record of her having talked to a detective, and most people—even a cop—would find being questioned in connection with a homicide probe hard to forget.

"No, I'm thinking that I *did* talk to a detective," she said. "What division was it?

"Van Nuys."

"Mmm . . . you know, I'm thinking that I did speak to somebody."

"Oh, really?"

"I couldn't tell you who it was. . . . He called me on the phone."

"Would it have been somebody in regards to this?"

"I don't even know if he said the name or if I would remember it, because I worked Van Nuys for a while. . . . But, yeah, I think I talked to somebody."

*   *   *

Nels never gave up, and he also never got anywhere.

He did get into it with John's dad more than once over John's refusal to sit down and discuss the facts of the case with him in detail. He and his wife put up a $10,000 reward, and cooperated with the producers of the TV show *Murder One*, which put together a segment about the unsolved case. He kept after LAPD detectives over the years, calling from Tucson, asking always if they had checked out the "lady cop." When he read the first stories about DNA testing in crime labs a few years later, he called and urged the department to run tests on the forensic evidence gathered from the condo and from Sherri's body. There were blood and hair samples, and there were swabs taken from the bite mark on Sherri's arm. He was told that the department had a limited budget and could not afford to run such tests, so Nels offered to pay for the tests himself. He even had a lab willing to do the work. He was told that the DNA would do them no good without a suspect. But, Nels insisted, he *did* have a suspect.

In fact, the department seemed determined to keep him from testing his theory. A detective named Phil Moritt visited the LA County coroner's office, in the Mission Junction district, on October 11, 1993, more than seven years after the murder and not long after Nels had requested a DNA test, and signed out all of the forensic evidence that might have contained a suspect's DNA. It is not unusual for a detective to remove evidence and deliver it for testing to a lab, and sometimes such errands involve fetching evidence from several case files. So there is no way to know whether Moritt sought only the Rasmussen material on this trip. Ordinarily such evidence is removed at the request of an investigator, but there is no record of such a request. Moritt would later tell department investigators that he had no memory of signing out the evidence. It was never returned. It is still missing.

Lazarus was promoted to detective that year. She worked in Van Nuys, as did Moritt. It is likely that they knew each other.

For eighteen years Sherri's file and what was left of the evidence from the scene of her murder sat in storage. Mayer retired. In 1989, John was reunited with Stephanie on a scuba-diving trip to Hawaii. Before he met her there, he told investigators, he called Mayer to make sure no evidence had ever linked her to Sherri's murder. It is interesting that the possibility, which he had so strongly rejected years earlier, remained in his mind. As he would recall it later, Mayer had assured him there were no suspicions about Lazarus whatsoever. Notes about that conversation are not in the Rasmussen file. So the lady cop and the widower reconnected in Hawaii. Lasting romance did not rekindle. John remarried some years later, and he and his second wife started a family. Lazarus married a fellow cop. She continued to rise in the ranks.

And there things would surely have remained, except . . .

In 2001, LA Police Chief Bernard C. Parks, created the Cold Case Homicide Unit to begin systematically combing through unsolved murder files for DNA evidence. With growing databases of genetic signatures on national computer files, such evidence could be instantly checked against the DNA profiles of millions of known criminals, greatly magnifying the potential return in mining such data. Investigators with the unit sift through stored evidence, looking for samples of blood, semen, saliva, and hair believed to have come from the murderer.

In 2004, Jennifer Francis, a criminologist with the cold-case unit, pulled Sherri's case and began sorting through the evidence. This was a matter of routine, but everything else that happened is not.

Life resonates after death, in the memories and affections of loved ones, and a strong character, an impressive one, sends out wider ripples. Sherri's file could not have failed to touch Francis. Here was a beautiful, brilliant, accomplished young woman, newly married and in love, surprised in her home and killed. And her killer had gotten away with it. Francis was certainly perplexed by Sherri's case. When she went looking for potential DNA in the case file, she discovered the record of Moritt's 1993 withdrawal. All the forensic samples that might have revealed the killer's DNA were missing. But when she looked closer, comparing the carefully enumerated list of evidence with the items that Moritt later signed out, she noticed that swabs taken from the bite mark on Sherri's arm had not been recorded, and yet they too were gone. They apparently had been misplaced sometime earlier, before Moritt's visit. Where might they be?

Francis knew well the steps in the evidence chain. Evidence recovered from the victim's body would be held for a time in the coroner's freezer, while the case was still active, and at some point would be gathered up and stored under the file number. What if the swabs hadn't made it from the freezer to the file? Francis called the coroner's office. The swabs were not on file, so they searched the freezers by hand.

The swabs were found in a padded manila envelope that had absorbed moisture from the freezer walls, and over time the corner of the envelope with the case number on it had worn away. It still had "Rasmussen" written on its front very clearly, but evidence is stored by number, not by name. Finding the number from the name would have required more work, so apparently whoever gathered up the forensic evidence years ago had avoided the extra effort and just left the envelope in the freezer, where it sat for eighteen years. Inside the envelope was a screw-cap test tube, and inside the tube were two swabs.

Francis sent the swabs to the lab for testing and got the results back in late January 2005. She ran the DNA signature through CODIS (Combined DNA Index System), the national law enforcement database, but there were no hits. However, the test results had shown something curious. The bite on Sherri's arm had been made by a woman.

Francis took this result back to the cold-case detectives, pointing out that if Sherri had been attacked by a woman, it upended Mayer's theory that she had been killed by two Latinos burglarizing her condo. This was how she saw it, anyway. The detectives did not agree. What if one of the two the burglars had been female? It wasn't typical—very few women are arrested for breaking and entering—but it also wasn't impossible. In any event, there were no female suspects in the file, and the point of the DNA project was not to reinvestigate every cold case but to see if the genetic material matched a known suspect. The evidence and Francis's revelation, much to her chagrin, went back into the box and back into storage, presumably forever.

Or at least for four more years, until the day after Super Bowl Sunday, 2009.

LAPD homicide detective Jim Nuttall came into work that morning, Monday, February 2, with a hangover. He and his brother, Steelers fans, had celebrated Pittsburgh's championship a little too aggressively the night before, so Nuttall decided to ease slowly into his workday. Instead of getting out in the streets to work on a current case, he fetched a cup of coffee and decided to spend a few hours at his desk, reviewing one of the cold cases that he had been assigned.

In recent years, murders had fallen off precipitously in Los Angeles, so detectives in the homicide units throughout the city had been given cold cases to review on top of the current murders they were working. Unsolved cases were routed to working detectives for one final review before they were closed permanently. Nuttall had a row of "murder books," as they are called—thick blue binders full of notes, photos, diagrams, transcripts. Just inside the binder cover is a progress report, a detailed account of everything that has been discovered about the case to date.

Right away, Nuttall saw the same contradiction that had struck Jennifer Francis.

In the interview room, Detective Jaramillo returned to the question of whether Lazarus had ever been to John and Sherri's home.

"I don't think I've ever gone there," she said. "I don't want to say I've never gone there and [have you say] I was there at a party. Like I said, I don't think so."

"But it's safe to say that the only time you would have been there was for something social?" asked Stearns.

"Something social. Yeah . . . I don't even know that I knew where they lived."

"But you didn't have any issues with her, right?" asked Jaramillo.

"No," she said, twisting up her face at such a preposterous suggestion. "But, I mean, if he were dating me and dating her, I probably said, 'Hey, pick,' or something. I can't say that we ever screamed or yelled. I mean . . . he was a pretty mellow guy. You know, I think I was pretty mellow. I don't think we had some big huge blowup . . . I was probably going out with other guys, and he was probably going out with other girls."

"I mean, would you remember if she snapped on you, like, 'Hey, that's my man. You know, leave him alone, blah-blah-blah,' that kind of stuff? You would remember an incident like that."

"Well, you know, and maybe that happened," she said, "Gosh, it's been so long ago. I mean that's not ringing a bell. . . . I'm crazy," she said, giggling nervously. "People think I'm really hyper, and I can get upset, you know, and, I mean, I forget five seconds later."

"Water under the bridge," offered the detective.

"I enjoy the job. I get excited. I've always enjoyed the job."

"You've got a good gig."

Whenever Lazarus found herself on dangerous ground she would pull back to talk again about The Job, the original premise of this conversation, just one cop pitching in to help her brothers. But the more she talked, the deeper her involvement in the story grew.

"Like I said, this stuff has been so long ago," she repeated. "I'm sure as soon as I walk out of here, I'll go, 'oh, shoot,' twenty-five things I'll remember."

"But you'll call us, or, I mean, you'll just come over to our desk and help us," suggested Jaramillo.

"I don't know what else you need to know. Like I said, we knew friends together. A lot of the friends that we socialized [with] in the dorms, there was a group of us that we were all really close. . . . We all did stuff together, after we all graduated, we went to weddings . . ."

"But Sherri wasn't part of this circle?"

"No, I don't even know how he met her; I don't know where they met. . . . He may have told me. That's not ringing a bell . . . I don't know what else to tell you."

"Well, one of the concerns I had, just looking at some of the notes, is some of Sherri's friends said that you and her were having a problem because of the John situation."

Lazarus puckered up her face and chuckled. In a while, Jaramillo came back to the subject again.

"You know what, I just can't say," Lazarus said.

"You can't say?"

"No, that doesn't even ring a bell."

"I mean, it seems like you actually would recall something if somebody's going off on you, right?"

"I mean, I would think. I would think . . ."

"And from what you're telling me is, when you guys met at the hospital, when you guys talked, that it wasn't, from what you recall, confrontational on either side?"

"I mean, I'm trying to turn my memory back," Lazarus said, twisting her hands on either side of her head as though rewinding a spool. "And I can't even picture the conversation."

"Well, let me ask, at the hospital it never got to a point where people were going, 'Hey, hey,' you know, or 'Everybody go to your own corner' type of thing?"

"I don't *think* so."

"Nothing like that?"

"I don't think so. I mean, I really don't. If you say people said that, that's not ringing a bell to me at all. I mean it's not."

"How about ever going to her house and having a dispute like that?"

"If I met her ever at his apartment, maybe I could've met her at the apartment. I'm thinking that the hospital thing, that sounds familiar, that I met her there. I just can't say that I've ever—again, was I there with other people? I don't know. I don't think I ever met her there or him there, meaning one or the other. I don't think so."

"Because I know how my wife is. I know she wouldn't want my girlfriends there, you know, so I don't know if maybe she had the same mentality toward you, as far as you not being welcome there."

"You know what, if somebody said I was there when they were there, then that's possible, but I just don't recall. I mean, I don't think so. It's not sounding familiar."

Studying the murder book, which has dozens of photographs of every relevant piece of evidence found at the crime scene, Detective Nuttall saw a different story than the one Mayer had pieced together. He had been so struck by the finding that the suspected killer was female that he reported it to his supervisor, Detective Robert Bub, who assigned two other detectives, Marc Martinez and Pete Barba, to help Nuttall completely rework the case. As they saw it, Sherri had not surprised burglars working downstairs. She had herself been surprised upstairs by the armed intruder. That's where the fight seemed to have started.

The front door had apparently been unlocked—Mayer had been right about that—and the alarm system was off, so Sherri would not have heard anyone entering stealthily. Two shots had been fired upstairs, and both rounds had gone through the sliding glass door, shattering it. The glass was bowed slightly outward, consistent with rounds traveling in that direction. It appeared to Nuttall that whoever had come looking for Sherri that morning had come to kill her. One round, probably the first shot fired, had gone clean through her chest and then out through the glass door. Once hit by that round, she had begun bleeding internally and had only minutes to live. Given Sherri's training as an emergency-care nurse, she may well have known that. But in the first moments she would still have had strength, and she appears to have used it to grab the gun and wrestle it away. The other shot through the door was low on the glass, consistent with a shot fired during a struggle over the weapon.

Sherri got the handgun, but instead of shooting her attacker, she ran down the stairs with it, apparently heading for the panic button on the security panel inside the front door. The killer pursued her. Smear marks on the walls along the stairs suggest that Sherri was spitting up blood into her hands, which then marked everything she touched, thus tracing her path clearly. The killer appeared to have caught her from behind on the first floor, where there was a violent struggle. Sherri was most likely pulled away from the wall panel. Her fingernails were broken, and there were blood marks on the floor in the foyer suggesting that Sherri had been dragged into the living room. Now she would be weakening and feeling dizzy, but with enough strength to wrestle with the killer— the bite mark on her forearm suggested that she managed to put the killer in a headlock. Escaping Sherri's grasp, the killer grabbed the heavy gray ceramic vase off the living-room shelf and crashed it hard into Sherri's forehead. She went down now for good. At that point Sherri's wrists were bound with the wire and cord found on the floor in the foyer. Using the pink and pale green blanket to muffle the sound, the killer then fired two more rounds into Sherri's chest, finishing the job. The cords were removed from her wrists and discarded.

Once Nuttall had thus reframed the confrontation, the evidence of burglary that had convinced Mayer looked like a deliberate attempt to mislead. The bloody smudge on the top of the disc player was telling. It would prove to be Sherri's blood, left by someone wearing a glove, which likely meant it had been gathered and stacked *after* Sherri was killed. The coroner had determined that she had been killed at about eight o'clock in the morning, which meant the condo had been perfectly silent until John returned home that evening. If the killer had panicked and fled after shooting her, which is entirely plausible, why would she go around the condo looking for things to steal, and then leave them stacked on the floor? The drawer in the living-room side table had been pulled out and left leaning against the legs, with the contents relatively undisturbed. What it looked like to the Van Nuys cold-case detectives was an effort to make the scene *look* like a burglary.

The killer had then gone out through the inside living-room door to the garage and driven off in Sherri's BMW. That was how the detectives, at least initially, pieced together evidence from the crime scene. Jennifer Francis's DNA work showed that Sherri's killer was most likely female. At the very least she had fought with a woman shortly before she was killed. The execution shots suggested that whoever shot Sherri was determined to kill her. So, the Van Nuys detectives wondered, what woman in Sherri's life wanted her dead and would have the presence of mind to alter the crime scene sufficiently to fool a busy LAPD homicide detective?

They noted in the comprehensive murder book, that on November 19, 1987, Mayer had noted, "John Ruetten called.

Verified Stephanie Lazarus, PO, was former girlfriend." What did "PO" mean? When they guessed "police officer," they ran the name through the department directory and came up with their esteemed colleague in the art-theft division.

Nuttall and Martinez went to see John Ruetten. "You have this information already, detective," he told them. John said that Stephanie had been Nels Rasmussen's suspect, but that he had never believed it. He still refused to believe it. The detectives next called Nels, who, after twenty-three years of getting nowhere, was understandably annoyed even to be asked the question. How many times did he have to tell them about Stephanie Lazarus?

With those interviews done, full of information that both supported and attenuated the Lazarus theory, the detectives drew up a list of six women who knew Sherri well enough to possibly have had a motive to kill her. They excluded no known possibility. The list included Sherri's mother and sister. Lazarus was number five.

They had the bite-mark evidence. The DNA from that swab, they strongly suspected, was from the killer. One by one the other five women were ruled out. The detectives obtained DNA samples from them—in one case surreptitiously, by rooting through trash—and in each case the sample didn't match. That left Lazarus, whom they were loath to accuse. If they were right it would cause a stink in the department, and if they were wrong they would needlessly smear a prominent fellow detective—a move bound to have adverse consequences for them. Still, the facts about number five kept adding up alarmingly well.

The detectives tried to imagine how a cop might go about planning to murder someone. She wouldn't do it on duty; she would do it on a day off. Lazarus had been off work on the day of the murder. A cop would be careful. She would wait until the victim was alone. If Sherri had been killed at about eight that morning, that means whoever did it had waited until John left for work (at 7:20 a.m.), and made sure he wasn't coming right back before heading into the house. After the murder, she would want to leave the scene in a way that minimized the chance that she would be seen clearly enough to be identified; the killer had entered the condo's garage from the inner door and driven away inside Sherri's BMW.

Then there was the murder weapon. Martinez said he doubted that a cop would plan to commit murder with her duty gun. You would want to get rid of it afterward, and there is hell to pay in the department for losing a duty gun. The Van Nuys detectives knew that most cops have at least two weapons, a duty gun and a backup, purchased privately and duly registered. Records showed that Lazarus had purchased a .38 caliber Smith & Wesson soon after graduating from the police academy. Martinez suspected that she would have gotten rid of it after the murder. If she became a suspect, the first thing her investigating colleagues would ask to see was both guns.

It would look very suspicious to say, "I don't know where it is" or "I lost it."

That wouldn't do.

"Were you like one of those young cops, like, 'Oh, I got a paycheck!' and bought a new car?" Jaramillo asked Lazarus.

Stearns and Jaramillo's conversation with their colleague bobbed and weaved. The detectives would zero in on something touchy and then back off into comfortable banter. Lazarus no doubt recognized the technique. They were toying with the idea that she had killed Sherri Rasmussen, but she still didn't know how serious they were about the notion, how much they thought they knew. As long as the conversation continued, there was still a chance she could lay their suspicions to rest.

"Oh, no. I've only had like a few cars my whole life," she said.

"So what did you have when you came on the job?"

"Well, my first car was a sixty-eight Chevelle; then I had a Toyota. Some type of Toyota. Hatchback, but I forgot what the name of it was."

"Like a Corolla or a Tercel? Something like that?"

"Tercel. Tercel. And then my truck."

"Were there any policies on it?"

"Like what?"

"Was there any general car-wreck thing? Stolen?"

"No, my car's never been stolen. Broken into . . ."

"Tell me about this car being broken into."

"My car's been broken into several times."

"Oh, really? Did you ever lose anything?"

"Yeah, now that you mention it. Let's see. I had a gun that was stolen. I had other stuff that was stolen."

"It's not your duty gun, was it?"

"No."

"Good. Was it ever recovered?"

"I don't know. I don't think so. Not that I know of."

The Van Nuys detectives had made a request to have the serial numbers of Lazarus's backup Smith-Wesson traced. Nuttall and Barba were driving through a dust storm south from San Francisco when they were called with results. When they heard, they pulled over to the side of the road to let it sink in. Lazarus had reported the gun stolen to the Santa Monica Police in March of 1986.

Often when circumstantial evidence begins to mount in a case, there arrives one key piece evidence pushes suspicion to certainty. The stolen-gun report was that piece of evidence. The timing was just too convenient for it to be a coincidence. The fact that Nuttall, Martinez, and Barba had been able to predict it added weight. By now they had also noticed the convenient absence of key records in the file. It sure looked as if someone inside had been working to protect Lazarus. This was going to be big. If ever a man had reason to be angry at the LAPD, it was Nels Rasmussen.

There is a set procedure in-house for investigating a fellow police officer. You first report it up your chain of command. But the detectives did not want anyone in their Van Nuys office to know about it yet; information tends to travel fast in-house. Nuttall, Barba, and Martinez had taken to referring to Lazarus simply as "number five" in their work. They phoned their supervisor, Detective Bub, at home.

The information went straight up the chain of command. Bub went to his commanding officer, Lieutenant Steven Harer, who went to the area commander, Captain William Eaton. Eaton directed Bub to meet with Deputy Chief Michael Moore. Everyone agreed: the investigation was solid. It was time to get a DNA sample from Lazarus. Moore authorized the deployment of the Internal Affairs Group's Special Operations Division to help.

They decided to do it surreptitiously, in order to avoid tainting Lazarus with suspicion if the lab test cleared her. A special operations team staked out Lazarus and her daughter on a trip to

Costco and recovered a cup and straw after the pair had snacked at a table outside the store. Two days later the lab confirmed that the mouth on that straw was the mouth that had bitten Sherri Rasmussen's forearm in a violent struggle twenty-three years earlier.

The decision to take Lazarus downstairs in the Parker Center for questioning before arresting her was made for two reasons. Officers have to check their weapons before entering the downstairs jail; the detectives wanted to avoid some kind of armed standoff if she flew off the handle. Lazarus was known to have a temper. They also wanted to gather further insight into what had happened before letting her know what they knew.

Lazarus was still smiling and chatting jovially with the detectives an hour into the interrogation. If she was annoyed, she was doing a good job of not showing it.

"Well, like I said, we're looking at the case. We've read the notes as far as Sherri's friends saying you guys had problems or words and it got heated," Jaramillo said. "The reason we are asking you is, there was an incident at her work that occurred, and they also told us that [there was] an incident at her house."

Lazarus screwed up her face comically, as if to say, *Whatever.* She threw up her hands.

"You know what?" she said, shaking her head and smiling. "That does not sound familiar at all. Again, if someone says I was at her house and I had an incident with her? That just doesn't sound . . . Was John there? Did John say this happened? And other people were there? I just don't recall. It just doesn't sound familiar."

"This was an incident where you showed up, you weren't supposed to show up, and things got heated."

Jaramillo was now referring directly to the murder. The detective was actually offering Lazarus something here. Was it possible she showed up just to talk to Sherri, and they got into it verbally—and then physically? That would be bad enough, but manslaughter is not the same as cold, premeditated murder. She did not take the opportunity.

"At his house? That just doesn't sound familiar. You know, it's not sounding familiar. Not at all."

"So it's not sounding familiar because you don't remember?"

"You know what? I have to say 'I don't remember' because I don't remember. It doesn't sound familiar."

"Would you not remember something like that in your life?"

"Well, I would think, but—"

"I mean the drama involved in, you know, the other-woman type of thing?"

"Did you ever fight with her?" Stearns asked.

"Have we ever fought?"

"Yeah. Did you ever duke it out with her?"

"No! I don't think so."

"You would remember *that*, right?" said Stearns. "That would be pretty—"

"Yeah, I would *think* so. Like I said, honestly, it just doesn't sound familiar. I mean, what are they saying? So I fought with her, so . . . I must have killed her? I mean, come on."

Lazarus continued to deny any memory of fighting with Sherri Rasmussen, contorting her features dramatically to express her astonishment. "That just sounds crazy to me," she said.

"OK, well, this case, you know, this occurred in eighty-six, right?" said Jaramillo. "The detectives processed the scene, things of that nature. They did fingerprints and all that stuff. You know, the standard things. You've been doing this longer than I have."

"I don't know about that. I've got twenty-six years on, going on twenty-six."

"But, you know, they processed everything. They did the best they could at that time, and they looked at a lot of people and different things in this case."

Lazarus caught his drift.

"If you guys are claiming that I'm a suspect, then I've got a problem with that, OK," she said, her tone changing sharply. She was finished with collegiality. "So if you're doing this as an interrogation, and you're saying, 'Hey, I'm a suspect,' now I've got a problem. You know? Now you're accusing me of this? Is that what you're saying?"

"We're trying to figure out what happened, Stephanie," said Stearns.

"Well, you know, I'm just saying. Do I need to get a lawyer? Are you accusing me of this?"

"You don't have to. You're here of your own free will."

"I know, but I mean—"

"You're not under arrest, you can walk out," said Jaramillo.

"You can leave whenever you'd like," said Stearns.

She did not leave. She listened, stern-faced now, as Jaramillo explained that detectives, as she well knew, had to consider every angle.

"Now, what we'd like to do is . . . If we asked you for a DNA swab, would you be willing to give us one?"

"Maybe," she said. "Because now I'm thinking I'm probably going to need to talk to a lawyer." Lazarus grew indignant. "I know how this stuff works, don't get me wrong. You're right, I have been doing this a long time. I wish I had been recording this, because now it sounds like all these people saying I was fighting with her. Now you sound like you are trying to, you know . . . I've been doing this a long time, OK, and now it all sounds like you're trying to pin something on me. I get that sense."

"You know it as well as we do," said Stearns. "Our job is to identify and eliminate suspects."

"I can't even believe this," said Lazarus, shaking her head slowly and leaning it down into her open left hand.

Jaramillo told her that he "may have" some DNA from the crime scene.

"That's great," she said.

"And we are going to do what we can to put this to rest," he said. "Your name is in the book; these people are pointing at you, for whatever reason."

"I don't know why. That's just crazy. I mean, that's absolutely crazy."

"And it would be irresponsible on our part not to look at it."

"I know. You guys have to do your job, and I guess I'm going to have to contact somebody."

"That's fair," said Stearns.

"Because I know how this stuff works. I just can't believe it."

"We understand that. If we were in your position, we would feel the same way."

"I just can't even believe it," she said, muttering to herself now, and then she looked back up at Jaramillo. "I mean, I'm shocked. I'm really shocked that someone would be saying that I did this. We had a fight so I went and killed her? I mean, come on."

She stood up abruptly, thanked the detectives for giving her "the courtesy" of discussing it with her, and walked out of the interview room, apparently believing that she really was free to go. She got as far as the hallway, where she was formally arrested and handcuffed.

She kept repeating, "This is crazy. This is absolutely insane."

Stearns read her the Miranda rights.

"Do you want to talk to us right now?" he asked, when he had finished.

"No," she said. "This is crazy. I'm like in shock. I'm totally in shock."

In March 2012, Stephanie Lazarus was convicted of the murder of Sherri Rasmussen and sentenced to twenty-seven years. In court, prosecutors interpreted the sequence of events during the fatal encounter in a way that slightly differed from the detectives' reading of the evidence in the summer of 2011 (when this story was written), but the accounts added up the same way. Lazarus had entered the condo and surprised, fought with, and then killed Rasmussen. The Rasmussens sued the LAPD, alleging that key evidence that pointed to Lazarus was removed from the file, but lost the case. According to Detective Stearns, an internal investigation of the missing evidence did not support the claim that anyone inside the department had deliberately covered up her involvement.

The Body in Room 348

Vanity Fair, May 2013

G reg Fleniken traveled light and lived tidy. After so many years on the road, he would leave his rolling suitcase open on the floor of his hotel room and use it as a drawer. Dirty clothes went on the closet floor. Shirts he wanted to keep unwrinkled hung above. Toiletries were in the pockets of a cloth folding case that hooked onto a towel rack in the bathroom. At the end of the day he would slide off his worn brown leather boots and line them up by the suitcase, drop his faded jeans to the floor, and put on lightweight cotton pajama bottoms.

Most evenings he never left the room. He would crank up the air-conditioning—he liked a cool room at night—and sit on the bed, leaning back on two pillows propped against the headboard. Considerately, to avoid soiling the bedspread, he would lay out a clean white hand towel, on which he placed his ashtray, cigarette pack, lighter, BlackBerry, the TV remote, and a candy bar. He smoked and broke off candy bits while watching

TV. This is what Greg was doing on the evening of Wednesday, September 15, 2010, in room 348 of the MCM Eleganté Hotel in Beaumont, Texas—lounging, smoking, snacking on a Reese's Crispy Crunchy bar, sipping root beer, and watching *Iron Man 2*.

He missed the ending.

Greg was accustomed to solitary nights. As a young man he had worked as a chief engineer on oceangoing vessels, spending months at sea. In middle age he had reinvented himself as a landman, a familiar occupation in South Texas, easing the exploitation of mineral rights on private property for gas and oil companies. Slender, with a close-cropped white beard and the weathered skin of a lifelong outdoorsman, he had partnered with his brother, Michael, in a thriving oil-land leasing business based in this small city east of Houston. Every Monday morning he would make the two-hour drive in his pickup from Lafayette, Louisiana, heading west on Interstate 10 through scruffy Gulf Coast farmland broken only by cell-phone towers, oil derricks, and billboards advertising motel chains and bayou restaurants, "Adult Superstores," and other local attractions. It took him through the stink of the big ConocoPhillips refinery at Lake Charles, a forest of piping, giant tanks, and towering chimneys. The hotel was just off the cloverleaf outside of Beaumont. He made the same drive in the opposite direction every Friday. His home in Lafayette was more in the style of New Orleans than Texas oil country, a small stone château with outbuildings around a shady courtyard, a place his mother had built to house her antique store, and which she had operated as a bed-and-breakfast. The antiques business was gone, but Greg's wife, Susie, still rented rooms. It was a home rich with style and character—in contrast to the Eleganté, a step up from the standard roadside lodging but a small one. His company rented him a room in the three-story "cabana" wing, which wrapped around a small swimming pool framed with potted palms.

That Wednesday night, watching his movie, Greg got an e-mail from Susie shortly after seven. She was using a computer program to file for a tax extension. After she reported her progress, he wrote back, "You're doin' good, Babe."

At some point during the loud, computer-generated showdown at the end of his film, amid all the fake violence, Greg was struck from nowhere with a very real and shattering blow—a blow so violent it would blind a man with pain. He might have heard at the same time a loud pop but was hardly in any condition in those critical seconds to sort out what had happened. He managed to get off the bed and move toward the door before he fell face-first, legs splayed.

He was probably dead by the time his face hit the green rug.

The following morning, Susie Fleniken called Greg's office. Husband and wife usually spoke every morning, but he hadn't called. He wasn't answering his phone. When he failed to turn up at the office, two of his coworkers drove over to the hotel and knocked on his door.

There was no answer, so they got the hotel manager to open it. Their alarmed calls brought an ambulance and the Beaumont police. They found a middle-aged man dead on the rug, prone, with a spent cigarette cupped delicately between two stiff fingers of his left hand. Room 348 was stuffy and exceptionally warm. The man's skin color had gone grayish blue. There was a dark wet spot at the crotch of his blue pajama pants, but that wasn't unusual.

Detective Scott Apple showed up a little more than an hour later. He is a short and very fit man with graying hair that he wears combed straight up, in spikes. He is all cop. His wife had been a cop; he met her on the job. He was one of the assault-team leaders on the department's SWAT team—one those men who never stops working.

But there was little here to interest Apple. No sign of a break-in or struggle. Nothing disturbed in the room. No blood or obvious wounds. Fleniken's wallet was still in the back pocket of his discarded jeans and had a stack of hundred-dollar bills in it, so robbery wasn't a motive. Those staying in nearby rooms had heard nothing. As Apple questioned the neighbors, he told them it was probably a "natural-causes thing." Sad. He poked around in Fleniken's bags, looking mostly for pills, some clue to his collapse. There were none. Susie and Michael later told him that Greg never went to a doctor. He was a stubbornly independent man, suspicious of authority and unmoved by the modern passion for health and fitness. He did not exercise. He had chain-smoked his entire adult life and had the nagging cough to prove it. He neither drank nor ate to excess, but he did both freely. It was easy to conclude that his choices had simply caught up to him.

Susie was ready to believe it. She was shocked and grief-stricken, but she accepted that, for Greg, sudden death was a possibility. In fact, she took some solace in it. He had checked out on his own terms. Many times she had heard him remark, upon hearing of someone dying suddenly, "Lucky bastard. That's how I want to go."

And so he had.

At the hotel, the police saw the death as routine. A photographer snapped pictures to make a record of the scene, and the body was driven by a transport service to the office of the Jefferson County medical examiner for an autopsy. The only mystery here appeared to be medical, and it was likely a minor mystery at that.

Dr. Tommy Brown had a time-tested method. It took him forty-five minutes to conduct a postmortem exam, inspecting a body inside and out, measuring and weighing organs, all the while describing what he found and noting the metrics that fleshed out the official form. When he worked with a detective alongside, he would explain what he was seeing step-by-step and what he could deduce from what he saw. He was all business, crisp, efficient, and confident. He did everything fast; he even talked fast. After Brown retired, a year later, the new firm that took his place routinely took three hours to do the same procedure. Some would credit this to stricter standards, but there was also an argument to be made for experience. The doctor was thin and bald on top and had a spray of unruly white hair that enhanced his mad-scientist image. He was a local character, part of the legal landscape in Jefferson County, and a respected one. Where death was concerned, in this corner of Texas, Dr. Tommy Brown's word was law.

The circumstances of the man's death, as reported, were unremarkable. On the table before him was a fifty-five-year-old Caucasian male who appeared to be in decent shape. After methodical inspection, the only marks Brown found on the body were a one-inch abrasion on the man's left cheek, where his face had hit the rug, and, curiously, a half-inch laceration of his scrotum. This was interesting. The sack itself was swollen and discolored, and around the wound was a small amount of edema fluid. The bruising around it had spread up through the groin area and across the right hip. Something had hit him hard.

The story his innards told was startling and intriguing. When Brown opened the front of the torso he discovered a surprising amount of blood and extensive internal damage. A small quantity of partly digested food had been torn from the intestines. The doctor found small lacerations there and on the stomach and liver, as well as two broken ribs, and a hole torn through the right side of the heart.

The condition of the man's insides reflected severe trauma: it suggested that Fleniken had been beaten to death or crushed. Brown concluded that the wound to his genitals likely had been caused by a hard kick. He had also taken a blow to the chest so severe it had caused lethal damage. He would have bled out internally in less than thirty seconds.

On the official form, next to "Manner of Death," Brown wrote, "Homicide."

When he got this surprising news, Detective Apple called Brown immediately for an explanation. The doctor told him that the man in room 348 had suffered the kind of severe internal injuries he was more used to seeing in crash victims or in someone found crushed under a heavy fallen object.

There are not that many murders in Beaumont. Greg's was one of ten that year, which was about average. Most are not mysterious. Detective work was usually a matter of doing the obvious—interviewing the drunk boyfriend with gunpowder on his hands, or finding the neighborhood drug dealer who was owed money. A case like this was a once-in-a-career event. If you enjoy working a stubborn whodunit, which Apple does, then this one presented an exciting challenge. But the problem with the hard cases is that they are, indeed, *hard*. They can mean a lot of toil that leads nowhere. Apple is a dogged worker and a good investigator. He had plenty of experience, and unlike many cops who have been on the job for years, he cared. He had professional pride and real empathy for the victim's family and loved ones. Apple welcomed the responsibility. Over the next weeks and months, he chased down every angle he could imagine to explain the death of Greg Fleniken. It challenged him intellectually and emotionally. But about six months into it, he was stuck.

The physical evidence didn't add up. Unless Greg had been beaten to death elsewhere, and his body had been returned to the room and carefully placed on the rug, nothing about the scene added up to a violent crime. How does a man get beaten so severely about the stomach and chest that ribs crack, inner organs tear, and his heart ruptures, all without significant exterior damage to his torso? Other than the bruising and the cut at his crotch, Fleniken's outer body showed no signs of a beating. And how could such a rumble have taken place in the hotel room without a thing being toppled or even disturbed? Without anyone in adjacent rooms hearing a thing?

Video from the hotel's various surveillance cameras offered no obvious clues. Fleniken was observed arriving at the hotel that evening but not leaving, and there was no sign from video of the outer doors or elevators of a body being carried back in. Whatever had happened to him had happened there, on the third floor of the cabana wing. Perhaps the beating had taken place outside the room in the hall, but there were no cameras in the hallway to provide evidence.

And there was no answer to the all-important question: Why? Greg appeared to have had no enemies. Apple talked a lot to Susie. She had been in her twenties, a singer in a rock band, when she met Greg. She clearly adored him. She was a delightfully offbeat Southern belle, buxom and pretty and warm, and oh so deferential but also, in that time-honored Southern way, stubborn as a tick. She was heartbroken and furious at the same time. Greg was the nicest man she had ever met. He was so nice, she had married him *twice*—first when they were kids, and then, after parting ways for a number of years, again in middle age. When Susie first called him again after that separation, he'd said, "I've been waiting for you to call." They had been married the second time for fifteen years. He was honest and ornery and easy and, as Susie saw him, utterly lovable. He was so genuine that he found it hard to lie about anything. When they were home together, and she was trying to nap, and the phone rang, she would say, "Don't answer." But he would answer, and he could not bring himself to cover for her, to say, "She's not here." He would tell her, apologetically, "I can't lie. I don't lie." In the weeks after his death, and after Brown's startling finding, she would ask plaintively, "Who would kill the nicest, most nonthreatening, most truthful man in the world?"

Greg's brother and coworkers said that he had been universally liked in their company and had no history of any run-ins with colleagues or employees. He was not the sort of man who sought confrontation. When someone had to be laid off or fired, he left the unpleasant task to someone else. There was nothing irregular about him. His life at the Eleganté rarely intersected with anyone else's. He went to his room early in the evening and usually stayed there by himself until morning. Often he ordered room service, a club sandwich and a root beer, and ate in his room. Apple interviewed bartenders, waitstaff, and management. Greg had never been seen down at the bar. He did not get in arguments or fights. He did not socialize or drink or pick up women. There was no evidence of relationships with anyone who worked at or frequented the hotel. On the few occasions when Apple was told he had been seen with a woman, the witnesses invariably described Susie.

So this was not a drunk. This was not a philanderer or a man who got into fights. This was a decent, honorable, smart, and successful man whom people liked. The sort of man nobody would murder—yet someone had. Someone had beaten him until his ribs cracked and his heart burst. Through the fall and into the winter of 2010, Apple pursued a number of possibilities. Maintenance records showed that at some point early in the evening of his death, while cooking prepackaged popcorn in the microwave, Greg had inadvertently blown an electrical circuit. The outage had affected the adjacent room, 349, and the rooms directly underneath. Greg had called the front desk to report the outage, and had confessed his role sheepishly to the worker who came up to reset the breaker.

This led to two theories.

The first involved sex. The Eleganté maintenance man who had come to Greg's room happened to have a rap sheet as a sex offender. Might the puncture wound to the scrotum and the internal injuries have been caused by a long screwdriver—during some sort of bizarre and kinky assault? Apple spent a lot of time talking to the maintenance man and looking into his background, checking out his story of that night, and scrutinizing the time line. Nothing out of the ordinary came up, and this theory never advanced beyond wild suspicion.

The second theory involved a group of union electricians staying at the Eleganté, a number of whom had been in the room next door, room 349, on the night Greg died. They were in town for an extended stay, doing a job for an oil company. At night they tended to assemble in one another's rooms to drink. What if some of them had been partying next door when the electricity went out? Might one or more of them have knocked on Greg's door and, perhaps drunk and annoyed, exchanged words with and then assaulted him in the hallway? Could Greg, badly beaten, have returned to his room and then collapsed? Some of the electricians had been questioned on the day the body was found, when Apple considered the death to have been of natural causes, and none said they had any interaction with the man in 348.

Nine days after Greg's death, armed with this new understanding of how he had died, Apple and a colleague returned to the third floor of the cabana wing to question some of the same men again. This time he came with suspicion. He was wearing a hidden video camera. The electricians were friendly and appropriately curious.

"What happened to that guy, anyway?" asked Lance Mueller, a sharp-featured man with dark, thinning hair, dressed in a T-shirt and blue jeans, who was still staying in room 349, along with a roommate, Tim Steinmetz.

"Hell, I don't know," Apple said, honestly. "That's what I'm trying to find out. It was almost like something fell on him or something. We're just trying to see if somebody heard something or maybe if somebody knows somebody who heard something, or maybe if somebody messed with him."

"You're trying to figure it out," said Mueller.

"Yeah," said Apple.

Mueller and Steinmetz had nothing to offer. The two electricians said they had heard the man in the next room coughing when they had returned from the bar late that night, but they had no clue what had killed him. Mueller seemed as confused as Apple was about the idea of something crushing him.

"There's nothing in these rooms heavy enough," he said.

Down the hall, they found three more of the electricians—Trent Pasano, Thomas Elkins, and Scott Hamilton. The men were friendly and tried to be helpful. One said that when he had seen the body on a gurney in the elevator, he had first assumed it was caterers delivering a cake or a big food tray.

"That's a better thought," said Apple.

"I thought he died of a heart attack," said Pasano, who said he had been in the room with Mueller and Steinmetz that night but had not seen or heard anything unusual.

"That's what we thought," said Apple. "It looks like something fell on him."

Nothing. The electricians handed over their driver's licenses and gave Apple their cell-phone numbers. They would be in town for a few more months, if anything came up. Happy to help.

Weeks went by. Months went by. Apple worked any theory he could imagine. He considered the possibility that Susie had had her husband killed, and thought about looking into Greg's insurance arrangements. Seizing Susie's computer or phone records would have meant getting a search warrant and then working things out with Louisiana authorities, but that would have demanded probable cause, which he did not have. He considered Michael Fleniken, Greg's brother and partner. Might he have had some motive? There was nothing that even hinted at it. Could Greg have gotten in a car accident on the way to the hotel? Had he been accosted on the street and beaten up some time before? There was no evidence for any of these conjectures.

Apple did get one exciting break. He had a friend at the Drug Enforcement Administration (DEA), who agreed to have Greg's BlackBerry analyzed. Printouts of its calling record were delivered, showing the phone numbers of top-dollar prostitution rings, outfits that matched hookers with johns over the Internet. What if Greg had arranged to rendezvous with a prostitute and things had gone wrong? Killed during kinky sex? Killed by an angry pimp? Apple wasn't eager to explore this angle with Susie, but she kept calling him, asking what was going on. As this was the only thing he had, he finally told her about it. Susie was upset. She was also adamant. That was *not* her Greg.

And she was right. The DEA had given Apple the wrong printout. The one from Greg's device held no surprises. He was, it seems, exactly the man he appeared to be. Apple was back where he had started.

Who doesn't love a mystery solved? It creates order from disorder, salves our ache for moral balance. An unsolved case is like a stone in your shoe—it just rubs and rubs. The work becomes drudgery. All paths suggested by the evidence become familiar and fruitless. This is where the case of the body in room 348 was by the end of 2010. Scott Apple was stymied. He had plenty of more pressing and promising work on his desk. Still, he talked often on the phone to Susie and to Greg's brother. He was sympathetic and open to anything they suggested. Hoping to unearth something new, the family put up a $50,000 reward. It produced nothing. Then Michael hired a private detective from Houston, a former FBI man. Apple happily met with the man and reviewed the case with him. That was the last he saw of him. The guy would call from time to time to ask Apple if he had anything new. From Apple's perspective, the guy was just taking money from the victims. Susie went to a well-known medium— "It was *not* inexpensive," she later told me—and Apple obligingly parked his skepticism, took notes, and did what he could to follow up, even though he did not believe in supernatural detection, and the scenario the psychic delivered, involving a group of Mexicans in a car, was a distinctly unoriginal thesis in Texas law enforcement. Still, how could Apple be dismissive at that point? Especially after he had raised with Susie the hurtful and bogus suspicion of prostitutes and then had to admit his mistake? She was fed up with him, and he knew it. She considered him and the rest of his department to be amateurs. And how could he argue with that? He had nothing.

The matter of Greg Fleniken was bound for the cold-case files. It would be just another sad box of notes and evidence stored in the Jefferson County Court House.

Ken Brennan took Susie's call on the golf course. She was surprised that he picked up the phone himself.

"Ken Brennan speaking."

"Oh my God, you don't have a secretary?" asked Susie.

She was flustered. The detective had answered on the first ring. She could barely get the story out—Greg's death, the coroner's finding, the dead end. He asked her to send him some files; he'd take a look. She said she had been feeling under the weather, but she would try to pull together what she had, pronto, and send it off to him.

"Well," said Brennan, "you need to fuckin' take care of yourself."

Like everything Brennan says, this came in a thick New York accent and a voice that sounds like it's strained through a cubic yard of gravel. It was a no-bullshit, you-better-listen-to-me command that was all the more startling because he had said something tender. It endeared him to Susie immediately.

Brennan is a retired Long Island cop and former DEA agent who makes a good living as a private detective in Florida. That's why he was on the golf course in February. He's pushing sixty, still solid, ruddy, and stylish, in the South Florida manner. Blue-eyed, thick-necked, and ruggedly handsome, he is partial to lightweight short-sleeved shirts that show off his torso and big arms. He wears flashes of gold at the neck and wrist, and Celtic rings on several fingers. Brennan's hair is mostly white now and is combed straight back on the sides and straight up in the front, in a low-key pompadour, cocky but dignified.

Months earlier, not long after Greg's death, Susie's friend Kea Sherman had told her and Michael about Brennan. Sherman, a young lawyer, had grown close to Susie and Greg when she lived for a time at their bed-and-breakfast while she clerked for a judge in Lafayette. She had her own practice in New Orleans now, and sharing Susie's frustration with the investigation, she had hit upon the strategy of filing a lawsuit against the hotel as a means of pursuing the probe privately. She had read "The Case of the Vanishing Blonde," my article in *Vanity Fair* (December 2010) detailing Brennan's remarkable success in resolving a 2005 cold case that had stumped the police in Miami. Now, when the investigation seemed hopeless, Sherman brought up Brennan again.

"If you want to do something," she urged Susie, "you have got to call this guy, the one I told you about. Just find him."

Brennan can be found readily on the Internet and is asked to look into more cases than he can handle. People come to him with unsolved murders and disappearances. Often they see him as their last hope. He takes these people seriously and handles them gently. He usually offers to review crime-scene photos and a summary of the case for free before making up his mind. When he reads a file, he is looking for a case that intrigues him but also one where he thinks he might be able to accomplish something. If the victim is someone who, say, vanished without a trace years ago, and there are no leads, he'll pass—"I ain't in the business of giving people false hopes," he says. The Fleniken case appealed to him not only because of the mystery but also because there were so many avenues to explore—Greg's family and coworkers, hotel guests, the maintenance man who had been the last to see him alive. To Detective Apple, none of these leads seemed new anymore, but to Brennan, they were all new and potentially promising. He knew that a fresh pair of eyes was perhaps the most valuable thing he brought to an investigation.

Brennan visited Lafayette in April. He worked Susie over first, asking her a lot of hard questions about their relationship, about Greg's faithfulness, about insurance arrangements, satisfying himself that the wife had no clear motive to have Greg killed.

"Let me ask you one more thing," said Brennan. "Was there anything about the crime scene that didn't seem right to you? That seemed off?"

Susie told him that she was surprised that the room had been so warm when Greg's coworkers entered it the following morning. Her husband liked to crank up the AC at night. She said he liked to sleep in a cold room.

Then Brennan went home and made arrangements for a second trip, to Beaumont.

Apple came out to a sports bar to meet him. Brennan was wearing a silky T-shirt under a sport coat, gold around his neck. He loomed over the detective. The two men ate and talked. Brennan said he just wanted to spend some time getting to know Apple before they reviewed the case. He told the Beaumont detective what he always tells the cops he meets in his work: "Look, I'm not a maverick. I don't do things half-cocked. If I decide we're going to do this, we're going to do it as a team. There's nothing I'm going to do that you're not going to know about it, and there should be nothing that you're going to do that I don't know about. The one thing I won't do is fuck up your case. . . . I've been doing this a long time. But I also know that you're the guy in charge here, so it's your case."

Part of what was going on was Brennan checking out Apple. "I don't want to work with somebody I don't like," he told me. He prides himself on being able to read people very quickly. He liked the Beaumont detective.

It was mutual. As Apple would put it later, "Ken has good people skills."

The following morning, Apple picked up Brennan, and they visited the hotel room. There Apple showed Brennan the crime-scene photos and the autopsy results, and reviewed what he had done over the previous seven months. Brennan heard him out and then announced, with what he would later admit was overstatement: "I think I know how this guy died. I think I know

when he died, and I think I know who killed him. And I think I
know how we're going to catch him."

"Come on!" said Apple.

"Hear me out. I'll tell you what I think, but first I've got to
call the guy's wife."

He called Susie's cell phone.

"Your husband, was he left- or right-handed?" he asked.

"He was right-handed."

"And when he smoked, did he smoke with the cigarette in
his left hand or his right hand?"

"He always smoked with his right hand."

"You sure?"

"I'm positive."

Brennan hung up and explained his conclusions to Apple.
Susie had already told him how cold Greg kept his room. This
helped fix the time of death. As Brennan saw it, the air condi-
tioner had shut down with everything else when the circuit
breaker blew. That time was known. Hotel records showed that
the repairman had left Greg alive and well at eight thirty p.m.
The movie resumed, and apparently Greg forgot to flip the AC
back on. It would have taken a few minutes for the room to grow
warm enough for him to notice, and by the time it had, he was
dead. That's why he had been found in a warm room—as Brennan put it, "In September, it's hot as fuck in Beaumont, Texas."

The cigarette scotched the notion that Greg had been beaten
severely somewhere else, perhaps even just out in the hall, and
then returned to 348. A hallway scenario would have explained
why nothing had been disturbed in the room, but the cigarette
ruled it out. There was no way his attackers, returning him,
would have added the fine touch of cupping one hand under his

body and delicately placing a burning cigarette between his fingers. It was also unlikely, given the ruptured ventricle, that Greg would have had time to return to the room after such a beating and calmly light up before keeling over. More likely, Greg had lit this cigarette himself *before* whatever happened to him happened. If Greg was right-handed, why was the burned-out cigarette found in his left hand? As Brennan pieced it together, after examining the state of the room—the pillows against the headboard, the candy, phone, and ashtray laid out neatly alongside where he would have been sitting, watching his movie— Greg had gotten up from the bed and headed toward the door, shifting the cigarette to his left hand in order to grab the door handle with his right . . . and died in his tracks.

It was hard to see this making sense, but Brennan had learned to be patient. A crime was a puzzle. Every piece mattered. It was a mistake to let what you do not know race out ahead of what you do. You might construct a perfectly satisfying version of a crime, one that you could even sell to a judge or jury. Brennan had known plenty of cops and lawyers who would grow so wedded to a theory that they were willing to trim the facts to make them fit. But he was a perfectionist. If there was even one small piece that did not fit, the puzzle was incomplete. So he was willing to follow the evidence, even in unlikely directions. Even when the conclusions it suggested were absurd. Greg could not have been beaten to death in his room, the evidence suggested, and yet he had died there, and he had died quickly after sustaining his wounds. Somehow, that's what had happened. Despite his earlier pronouncement to Apple, Brennan didn't know yet exactly how it had happened, and could not yet imagine an answer, but he was convinced that Greg had been quietly minding his own business just minutes, even seconds, before he was killed.

This is what led to the electricians, who were close by. Their room had been partly blacked out by the blown circuit at the same time Greg's had been. Of all the scenarios Apple had considered, this was the one that made the most sense: the union guys, who may have been drunk, might have confronted Greg in the doorway, exchanged words, and kicked him to death right there. Brennan asked Apple if he had interviewed them.

"Yeah, they were nice," said Apple.

"See anything hinky?"

"No, no."

"I'm sure if they were drinking they had to talk about it to each other," said Brennan. "So somebody knows about them. Probably one or two of their close friends or their coworkers are going to know about this."

They next paid a visit to Dr. Brown. Brennan wanted to know if the injuries Brown had seen might have been caused by a severe beating. They might have, the doctor said. The laceration of the scrotum could have been caused by a hard kick, especially if the assailant had been wearing steel-toed boots or boots that had metal hooks to hold the laces. The electricians wore construction boots.

Brennan asked Apple to start interviewing men who had worked with the union electricians the previous summer. He returned home to continue inspecting the hotel's surveillance video. It was time-consuming work and not particularly helpful. He calls it "looking to see the to and fro." The cameras showed

Greg coming in from work that evening. They showed several of the electricians making trips to their vehicles in the parking lot. But there was nothing obviously suspicious.

When Brennan returned to Beaumont in late May, he and Apple went to see some of the electricians' coworkers who had not yet been interviewed. By this time the union electricians had been gone for seven months. Apple's efforts with their coworkers had uncovered nothing, but Brennan was convinced the pursuit was worthwhile. Human nature being what it was, if any of the electricians knew something about Greg's death, word would have spread.

So Apple and Brennan made the rounds. Yes, most of the men had heard about the man who died in the Eleganté Hotel. What a shame. Did anyone know yet what had happened to him? Everything these men knew was second- or thirdhand or worse, and the stories were, predictably, confused. As Ken would remember it later, one of the crew foremen, a man named Aaron Bourque, had heard something about a gun going off in a boardinghouse.

"No," Apple corrected him. "That's not the same case. This was the one where a man got in a fight at the Eleganté Hotel."

Bourque had heard nothing about that.

As they drove away from Bourque's house, Brennan said, "We need to go back to the hotel."

"What are we going back there for?" Apple asked, noting that he and Brennan had already inspected the room thoroughly.

"We're going to look for a bullet."

Apple pointed out that they were not investigating a shooting.

"Yeah, but this guy mentioned a gun. Any time somebody mentions a gun, you gotta check that shit out. Everybody remembers a piece of a story. But when somebody mentions a gun, that's the kind of thing you recall. That's the part of the story that isn't going to get changed."

Brennan believed that Greg Fleniken had been beaten to death right there in the doorway to his room. It had happened quickly. What if there had been a gun involved? Maybe these electricians believed they had shot Greg, even if they had not. Still, if a gun had gone off, there would be a trace of it in that hotel room.

So they got hotel security to let them back into room 348.

They opened up the blinds and began inspecting the floor, the furniture, the walls—everything. They both worked on their hands and knees, shining flashlights under furniture. They focused most of their effort around the doorway to the room, because that's where the fatal scuffle had likely occurred. They found nothing. Brennan was frustrated, convinced now that somehow a gun had been involved. They were about to give up when he noticed an indentation in the wall alongside the closed service door that opened into the adjacent room, 349. The indentation was a repair job. It appeared to be right where the doorknob would hit the wall when the door was swung open—typical wear and tear. But when he opened the door, the knob and the dent didn't meet. The doorknob touched the wall slightly to the right of the patch. Something else had damaged the wall at that spot. Even after the repair there remained a slight divot.

"Let's take a look at the other side," Brennan suggested. When they got into room 349, there was no mistaking what they found on the wall there: a small hole that had been amateurishly patched.

"That's a fuckin' bullet hole," said Brennan.

Brennan stood alongside the smaller hole in 349, measuring its height on the wall against his hip. Then he walked back to 348 and did the same thing. The marks lined up. The neat hole in 349 was an entry hole; the divot in 348 had patched an exit hole. The worker who had done the work on 348's wall had recorded what she found. There was no report of a repair job in 349. Someone had patched that hole with what looked like toothpaste. It blended so nicely with the color of the wall that unless you were looking for it, you would not see it.

"You got a forensics team?" Brennan asked Apple.

When Beaumont's lab crew showed up, they carefully excavated both holes and shone a laser through. The trajectory pointed straight to the bed where Greg had been sitting, smoking, eating candy, and watching his movie.

Brennan said, "This motherfucker was shot."

Dr. Brown was not convinced.

He had examined the man's body from head to toe, cut him open, inspected his inner organs one by one, and reversed the expectations of the police. With precision and with the insight of years, he had determined that Greg Fleniken had died not from natural causes but from a severe beating. Now they wanted to tell him, on the basis of some new theory, that his own careful and professional observations were wrong? That he had missed, of all things, a bullet wound?

Brennan had volunteered to do the talking. After he and Apple had found the bullet hole and traced the trajectory, the answer to the mystery of Greg's death was clear, he believed. But in order to act, in order to bring Greg's killer or killers to justice, they would have to get the coroner to rewrite his finding. You could not argue in court that a defendant had shot someone when the medical examiner's office had concluded the victim had not been shot.

"Do me a favor," Brennan asked Apple. "Let me handle this whole fuckin' thing. I know it's your investigation, it's your deal, but you've got to work with this guy from here on out, so if he gets pissed off or annoyed, I don't want him pissed off and annoyed with you. Let him get pissed off at me."

Brown's office was a mess. Papers, files, books everywhere—every available surface was buried, even the floor. Brennan and Apple cleared away space on two chairs to sit down, and when they mentioned they were working the Fleniken case, the doctor asked, "Oh, did you catch the guy that beat him up?"

"No, we're not there yet," said Brennan, and he started to explain what they had discovered, trying to approach the subject delicately. Brown quickly got the picture.

"You're trying to tell me that this guy was shot," he said. "I'm telling you, he wasn't shot." Showing he was already two steps ahead of them, he flatly refused to order the body exhumed. Exhumation is a pain in the ass. It is expensive, disturbing to the family, and a hell of a lot of work—not to mention, as he already had, *unnecessary*.

And, as it happens, impossible, since Greg's body had been cremated. The ovens were hot enough to destroy metal fragments—Brennan had checked. Maybe a mass spectrometer could find something in the ashes, but . . .

"Listen, Doc," Brennan proposed. "Let's just take out the photos from the autopsy and go through them and see what we can find."

Brown humored them. As they passed the prints back and forth across the medical examiner's desk, Brennan pointed out things.

"What about this here," he said, pointing at a spot of damage.

"Yes, that's the liver."

"And what about this here?"

"Yes, that's the intestines."

Brennan knew what he was looking at. The bullet had entered Greg's scrotum and torn up through his torso. The scrotum skin was soft and pliable, and it had folded over the entry wound, making what it was less obvious. The internal injuries traced the bullet's fatal trajectory. He asked, "Doc, could all of this damage been done—besides blunt-force trauma, could a bullet cause the same?"

"Yes, it could, but that's not what happened here. This man was beaten."

"OK, Doc, but could it have?"

Brennan found something in a photo that supported his argument, that looked like a track.

"You could get the same thing from being beaten," Brown persisted.

Then they got to the heart. Brown passed the photo to the detectives.

"Doc!" Brennan said.

"What?"

"That's a bullet hole, Doc."

Brown took the photo.

"What?"

Brennan pointed. "That's a fuckin' bullet hole."

Brown explained that sometimes when a person is kicked or hit with a blunt object in the chest, it is the right ventricle that normally bursts.

"Doc, that's a fucking bullet hole."

Brown looked again.

"Yeah, that's a bullet hole."

After a long moment he added, "The media is going to kill me on this."

Tim Steinmetz must have been feeling pretty OK about this meeting with the Texas cops. Getting called in had been a shocker. It was more than seven months since he and Lance Mueller had come home from the job in Beaumont. Now two cops from down there had come all the way to Wisconsin to see him and to question him about the guy who had died next door. It had been worrisome. He and Mueller had conferred about it beforehand by phone and made sure their stories were straight. Steinmetz met the detectives in an interview room at the Chippewa County Sheriff's Department, and, really, they could not have been nicer. Tim sat in a swivel chair on one side of a big wooden table, and they sat opposite him with their notebooks open and files handy, very official. They thanked him for coming in. They chatted with him about the hassles of driving cross-country in a broken-down pickup. Nice guys. They assured him that this was just routine. They just needed a statement from him, that was all, something for their files.

They walked him through the evening, asking a lot of questions, and Steinmetz answered diligently, trying to remember

every detail—leaving out the part about the gun, of course—
but, thank God, these guys did not push him *at all*.

"You heard that the guy next door to you died?" asked the
older one, the big guy with the white hair combed straight up
in front, Ken Brennan.

"We did hear that," said Steinmetz. "But we didn't know for
sure what was going on. . . . We had no idea. We didn't hear no
commotion next door, no banging or nothin'. That's why this is
kind of weird."

Brennan and Apple walked him through the whole thing,
taking notes. Then Apple wrote the statement out carefully, and
asked Steinmetz to go through it, read it out loud, and make any
corrections he wanted. He noticed that Apple had put down that
he was an "apprentice," so he changed that to "journeyman." A
few other little things. He initialed all the places where he made
a change. Then they brought in a local cop to notarize the statement right there in front of him.

"And that's it, huh?" Steinmetz asked.

"That's it," said Apple.

"You guys flew all the way here for that?"

So Tim was feeling pretty good when he stood up to go.

"Is that it?" he asked.

"Hang on a second," said Brennan. His tone was different
now, harsh. "It was OK until you signed that statement. Now
you've got a problem."

"OK," said Steinmetz, startled. He sat down again.

"Now tell us what *really* happened," said Brennan. "Because
we know what happened. Because now you're going to jail with
him. Do you want to go to jail with Lance?"

"Why am I going to go to jail with Lance?"

"You just made a false police report, that's why," said Brennan. "You want to go to jail for that?"

"Tim, we know what happened," said Apple, speaking more gently. "We know everything that happened down there. And I realize you are trying to be noble and protect your friend, but you are about to get your whole family in a bind, and it's just not worth it. It's not worth it."

"So, just tell us what happened," said Brennan. "Just tell us what happened. Or, if you want to go to jail with him, go right ahead."

"No," said Steinmetz.

Out came the whole story, corroborated later that same day, June 1, 2011, in an interview with Trent Pasano, who had been in room 349 with Steinmetz and Mueller. Between the two accounts, the following scenario emerged. The electricians had been drinking beer. Mueller had asked Pasano to fetch a bottle of whiskey from his car and to also bring up his pistol, a 9 mm Ruger. When Pasano returned, Mueller had taken the handgun and, to the others' alarm, started playing with it. He pointed it at Steinmetz, who dropped to the floor and cursed at him, and as he was pointing it in Pasano's direction, at the foot of the bed, it went off. Pasano thought for a second he had been hit, but then turned to see a hole in the wall behind him. Mueller freaked out, they both said. Pasano and Steinmetz quickly shut the sliding door overlooking the pool and pulled the shades, worried that any people down there would be looking up after hearing the loud pop. Mueller bundled up the gun and took it back out to his car in the parking lot. By the time he returned, Pasano had left for his own room, disgusted. Mueller and Steinmetz went downstairs to the bar.

Steinmetz said they had not known for sure there was anyone staying in the room next door until, as he remembered, they heard someone in the room coughing, very late, after midnight, when they came back from the bar.

He held nothing back. Steinmetz's second statement, the truthful one, laid out the whole thing. It was good to get it off his chest. When he and Mueller had seen the police in room 348 the next morning, and the gurney, they had been horrified. "I thought he had killed that guy."

The only detail that didn't fit was this business of the two electricians' hearing a cough behind the closed door when they returned from the bar. Neither Brennan nor Apple was inclined to place much weight on it for several reasons. If it were true, then Greg had survived the gunshot for far longer than the coroner believed possible, but it did not alter the cause of death. If anything, it made the electricians' failure to check on him or call for help all the more egregious. More likely, Steinmetz and Mueller had heard Greg coughing in the room the previous evening. They had been staying next door that night too and had been down at the bar until late. On both nights they had been drunk. Fixing the cough late on the night Greg died was the only shred of Steinmetz's story that contradicted the detectives' reconstruction, and he—and Mueller—would cling to it, even though it hardly mattered.

"Did anybody knock on the door to check on the guy?" Brennan asked.

"No," said Steinmetz. "I always ask myself, if I was in a situation like this, you know, what would I do, and I admit—"

He never finished the thought. The detectives had something else they wanted him to do.

"Hey, Lance, what's up?" asked Steinmetz. He'd dialed Mueller on his cell phone. Apple and Brennan were recording the call.

"Not much," said Mueller. "Just sittin' around."

"Well, I just got back from down there."

"How did it go?"

"Well, I told them the whole story. You know, what had happened, that we were stickin' to there, you know?"

"What's that?"

"You know, the story that we were stickin' to, that we got home late that night, you know, and the guy coughed or whatever."

"Right."

"And, uh . . ." Stenmetz began to hem and haw. "And, uh, I was fixin' . . . I was gonna leave there then, because your lawyer said it would be OK, right? You know?"

"Right."

"And when I left there, they said, 'OK, you know, tell us the truth.' So I, you know, I told them the truth, what really happened."

There was a long silence on the other end.

"About the gun going off and all that?" Mueller asked.

"Yep."

"What did they say?"

"Well, that I would be in trouble, you know, if I didn't tell them."

Another silence.

"So, what did they say?"

"Not much. I don't know if they are going to get ahold of you, or Trent, or what the hell they're going to do."

Mueller sighed heavily. Then he groaned.

"What did they mean by that? I mean, 'Tell us the truth'? Did they say anything about the gun prior to that or what?"

"No. They just said they knew exactly what happened. Told me to stop fuckin' lyin'. They were pretty pissed. And then I told them exactly how everything went down, and what really and truly happened." Steinmetz suggested that Mueller call Apple right away. "They are probably going to come and get your ass, now that they know the truth and everything. You should probably try and make some kind of effort, you know? . . . The guy, he died from the gunshot."

"Are you shittin' me, Tim?"

"No, I'm not."

"Oh my God, are you kidding me? Are you serious right now?"

"I'm serious as a heart attack, Lance."

Mueller refused to believe him. For the next few minutes of the call, he went around and around with Steinmetz. His lawyer had obtained the autopsy report and assured him that the man had not died of a gunshot. The story had been all over the news. "It doesn't make sense!" he said. "If there was a gunshot, if he was killed from, you know, a firearm, they would have said something on the damn news!" Mueller pointed out that the day Apple and the other detective had questioned them in their hotel room, the gun had been in a small cooler right on his bed. If they had been looking for a gun, why wouldn't they have searched the room? Hadn't they seen the hole in the wall? In the weeks and months since, he had worked hard to convince himself that the accidental gunshot and the death of the man in room 348 were unrelated—and the autopsy report had confirmed it.

"It doesn't make sense!" he protested. "First the coroner ruled that it was a heart attack. Then they started saying it was something fell on him. . . . There's no way! There's absolutely no way that guy was killed by a bullet!"

He asked Steinmetz how he was doing.

"How'm I doin'?" Steinmetz said. "Not good. I need to drink some more beers."

Mueller apparently applied the same remedy, because he later phoned Brennan, clearly intoxicated, and started trying to explain himself. He said he wanted to make a statement.

"You're drunk," Brennan told him. "I suggest you call your fuckin' attorney."

Brennan was worried when the judge started reading the sentence. He had flown to Beaumont on October 29, 2012, to join Susie Fleniken and Scott Apple and a group of Greg's family members and friends for the sentencing of Lance Mueller. The electrician had entered a no-contest plea to manslaughter. As Brennan remembered it, the judge began by saying that this whole tragedy might be seen just as a terrible accident.

Oh fuck, thought Brennan, *here it goes. Don't tell me this guy is going to get a year or something.*

But then the judge started cataloguing the long list of willfully irresponsible choices that had led to this day.

More like it, thought Brennan.

The judge gave Mueller ten years, half of what the law allowed. The apology Mueller offered in court, no matter how sincere, came way too late. There was his criminally irresponsible decision to drunkenly play with the gun. As Steinmetz had said, they had suspected from the start that this errant bullet had at least helped kill the man in room 348. Even a heart attack, which had been the first assumption as the police rolled his body out on a gurney, might have been triggered by the gunshot. Then, after the coroner ruled that Greg had died of blunt-force trauma, Mueller was happy to accept that something had crushed him to death, even if it was hard to imagine what. Still, he had been worried enough about the gunshot. He had himself patched the hole with toothpaste. He had hidden the gun immediately in his car, then stashed it with a friend for the first days after the incident, and then had handed it over to an attorney for safekeeping before he left Texas.

What a huge mistake. If he had come forward at any time prior to Brennan and Apple solving the mystery, which had taken about eight months, it is unlikely he would have been charged with any crime, much less gone to jail. Mueller had gambled from the start that whatever connection he had to Greg's death would never be discovered. The odds were his favor too. If Susie had not made that phone call to Ken Brennan, it's doubtful Mueller would have lost the bet. As it was, even after the connection to his gunshot was made, the county district attorney's office had been reluctant to prosecute the case as a felony.

Brennan had responded by confronting the DA when he found out that the prosecutor might opt for a plea deal. He had flown to Beaumont and joined a meeting between Apple and Paul Noyola, an investigator for the DA's office. Noyola explained that accidental gun discharges in Texas were not uncommon, that juries and judges tended to understand them, and that, well, the whole issue of accident versus manslaughter was a fairly gray area of the Texas criminal code. The gun was still locked in Mueller's lawyer's safe, Noyola said, and he was making noises about fighting efforts to turn it over. In other words, the whole thing was looking like more of a hassle than a slam dunk.

"I suggest you go down there with a search warrant and a fuckin' blowtorch and go get the fucking weapon!" Brennan said. "It's evidence of a capital crime. What the fuck are you talking about?"

The private detective was incensed. He arranged to bring Susie to Beaumont for a private meeting with the assistant DA in charge of the case. Here's what he remembers saying:

"The victim was important to everybody here," he began, gesturing around the table. "And we're not going to let this thing be brushed under the rug, [or] let somebody take a plea on this. This is not a fucking accident. An accident is when somebody comes in, has taken off their gun, their gun discharges, and God forbid, somebody is hit . . . That's one thing. It's completely different when somebody fuckin' brings a gun that they shouldn't have [Mueller had a prior conviction that Brennan assumed should have barred him from carrying a gun] into another fuckin' state, shit-faced drunk, fucking around with a gun. The people with him realize that something bad could happen. They make the guy unload it, put it in the car. Then he goes and gets another guy to bring it back in. He's fucking around with it, drunk again, and discharges a round. Almost kills the guy he's with. And then he *does* kill somebody on the other side of the wall. He knows that's something that could happen; it's an occupied hotel. He doesn't even bother to knock on the door next door to see if anybody's hurt. And after that, his answer to the whole thing is to go get drunk some more in the fucking bar of the hotel? And then when he sees a body being taken out the next day, and he is one hundred percent certain he killed somebody, he decides not to say anything about it but run to his attorney and leave the fucking weapon in a safe, and the fucking attorney doesn't say anything about it either? You know what that is? That's fucking murder. So if you think we're going to forget about this fucking thing, think again. Because that ain't fuckin' happening."

Brennan's anger can fill a room.

After Mueller was sentenced, Brennan and Apple went out for a celebratory lunch. Brennan ordered a cocktail. Apple, who was on duty, didn't. They made plans to play golf together.

In the courtroom that day, Susie Fleniken had had a chance to speak to Mueller directly.

"I have waited over two years to look you in the face, eye to eye, and simply have the chance to speak directly to you," she said. "You would never have come forward with the truth. . . . You murdered him. No, you didn't intentionally seek him out to murder him, but you murdered him, with every lie you told, with every intentional selfish deception, with every cover-up, over and over again. . . . You saw his body taken out of the room in a body bag the next day. You knew you killed him. He meant *nothing* to you."

Later, Susie told me that she watched Mueller's face as the sentence was pronounced and that he had looked terribly shocked. That was good, she thought. *He's shocked, but not as shocked as my husband was.*

That night in room 348, relaxing, smoking, watching *Iron Man 2*, Greg Fleniken could not have known what hit him in the moments before he died.

Mueller knew exactly what was hitting him.

"You have met your match," said the small woman, staring across the courtroom at him, a study in controlled ferocity. "I would have spent the rest of my life tracking you down. And I found you. Greg's murderer. I brought you to justice."

Who Killed
Euhommie Bond?

Air Mail, December 2019

Seven years before Ken Brennan took the case, before the
heartbreak and the false accusations and suspicions split
family and community in Jackson, Tennessee, it was a typically
frantic night at Spanky's Bar & Grill.

It was actually very early morning, on Sunday, December
7, 2008, when Angela Bond, seeing her husband enter, shot him
the evil eye.

Together Angela and Euhommie Ollie Bond owned the
place, housed in a square red-brick building with a windowed
front at one end of a small strip mall. Spanky's stayed open
until three in the morning and often filled in the wee hours
after other bars had closed. In the kitchen, Angela was working fryer baskets with both hands, trying to keep up with
orders, when she saw her husband out by the bar. Euhommie
Ollie Bond was a deputy with the Haywood County Sheriff's
Department. His duty shift had just ended, and he typically
dropped in near closing time. He had left his uniform shirt,

vest, and weapon in the car, and stripped down to a long-sleeved black undershirt.

Euhommie Ollie Bond, known to his family as "Homie" and to those in the community as "Ollie"—or "Chief" since he had served as police chief in nearby Bradford—was a man people noticed. A competitive bodybuilder, he was striking; he had once won a silly TV contest on *The Ricki Lake Show*, attaining the title world's most "desirable" man, which he enthusiastically embraced. He had a broad, square chin, a magnetic smile, and charm that he kept at full throttle. On each of his bulging deltoids was tattooed a big red rose.

Much of Bond's magnetism was directed at women, which had caused friction in his marriage, but on this night Angela's ire concerned something else. One of Bond's cousins, whom she had asked him to fire, had shown up again to work that night. It was too loud and too busy for her to raise the issue just then. The look said, *You and I will talk later.*

It was a conversation they would never have.

A fight started. Dustups were not unusual at Spanky's. People were drinking and some were using drugs. It was a loud loose crowd at the frayed end of a long Saturday night. There were friends and enemies, lovers and haters, romantic rivals, near and distant cousins, straying husbands—a potentially volatile mix of Jackson intimacies. Some patrons were armed—Jackson was home to at least three violent street gangs. Bond bridged many of these divides and managed to keep trouble at a low boil. Both host and bouncer, he was known to all, mostly well liked, and unintimidated by the clientele. His police credentials lent weight to his imposing frame. When the fight started that night he leapt over the bar to break it up. Angela saw her husband wrap his big arm in a choke hold around one of the combatants, while another cracked him over the head with a bottle. Blood ran from a cut over his right eye. Bond shouted for everyone to stay calm as he half-pushed and half-carried the man he held out the front door.

The brawl scattered the crowd. Some raced out to the parking lot, some retreated to back rooms and lavatories. Angela ordered the kitchen to halt work and, still holding two baskets dripping hot oil, raced to the cash register to protect the night's earnings. Then came gunshots. Angela felt something whiz past her, close, and dropped to the oily floor. Someone shouted, panicked, "Chief's been shot!"

One of Spanky's security guards, an old Bond family friend, Eric Cobb, raced in waving a handgun. He jumped on a table, bellowing—as Angela recalled it—"Where's the motherfucker at?"

Someone else shouted for her to call 911.

She had misplaced her cell phone. She found the bar phone and momentarily froze. By the time she gathered herself and dialed, the dispatcher told her that others had already called. Responders were on their way.

The shooting had stopped as suddenly as it started. The crowd was now mostly outside. Cars were pulling away, fleeing the scene. Angela found her husband in one of the empty parking spaces. Blood had pooled under him. One of her customers, Lawanda Williams, a nurse, had torn away his shirt and was working on him, trying to staunch the bleeding from his abdomen. He was unconscious.

"Baby, I've done all I can do," Williams told Angela. "Only God can pull him through from here."

The rest was a blur. When the police arrived, they stopped Angela and Euhommie's uncle, Wilbert Bond, from lifting him to a car and taking him to the hospital, which was just two miles away. The cops told her to calm down. Then the ambulance came.

Bond was still breathing when they took him away. He died in the emergency room a short while later. The round had severed a major blood vessel.

Debra Bond Perry, the victim's aunt, had always been partial to him. Even as a boy his personality was outsized. One of her older sister's seven children, he had, to Debra, stood out. His cheerful bravado and playful sense of humor matched her own, and he had a soft side that melted her heart. Not much older than her nephew, Debra had been like a teenage sister to Euhommie when he was a boy, but as her sister fell victim to Alzheimer's and was increasingly lost to them, the attachment became more maternal. If she had had children, Perry says, she would have wanted a son like Euhommie. She loved him, and she admired what he had made of himself, a husband, father, military officer, policeman, business owner. She was enormously proud of her nephew.

His peculiar name had been his mother's attempt at christening him after Muhammed Ali, and like the boxer, Bond was not shy about his gifts. Spanky's was just another stage for him; he would wade in late and take charge. Even though he never drank or used drugs himself, he loved to entertain those who did. He would invite a crowd over to his house for a football game, furnish drinks and snacks, and then fall asleep in his recliner as everyone else drank, ate, and watched the game. He was so assertively friendly that some found it off-putting.

"People either loved him or hated him," said Gwen Sanders, one of his sisters.

He showered compliments on women indiscriminately— old, young, fat, slender, pretty, and plain. At the drive-through window of a McDonald's, waited on by a young woman with bright blue hair—"She looked a hot mess," recalled Sanders— Bond had proclaimed, "You know, not everybody could do blue hair, but blue hair looks *good* on you." Beneath the come-on was genuine sweetness. When Perry's husband died, her nephew presented her with a video piecing together memories of his uncle with photos and music. He recorded an introduction while sitting on a bench in his weight room, shoulders and arms bare and tumid. Staring into the camera, he said, "Auntie Debra, I know that someone else should be doing this, not me, because this is for someone soft." The rest was unabashedly sentimental. She cherished it. Perry had been distressed when Euhommie and Angela bought Spanky's. "Nothing good will come of people drinking after midnight," she warned him. But it had proved to be a moneymaker, and Bond enjoyed it. He served drinks, flirted, held forth, and kept the peace. If Angela, backstage in the kitchen, was Spanky's producer, her husband was its star.

Bond's violent death was shattering for his family and for many in Jackson's African American community, a pain prolonged, year after year, by the police department's failure to catch his killer. Seven years on, his family's sadness had turned bitter.

"We were still grieving in a really bad way," said Perry.

She and Sanders had put up a $10,000 reward, half each, hoping to turn up some answers. Angela put up another $5,000.

They had posters placed on city buses advertising the reward. It hadn't helped.

"I'm a forensic person," says Perry. She's a forward woman of fifty-three with certain opinions and a barbed sense of humor. She admits to, with a trace of wicked delight, "a reputation in my family for speaking my mind and saying exactly what I think, which is, you know, not always a good thing." A retired postal worker—she says, without a trace of sarcasm, "the greatest job in the world; I *loved* that job"—she spends a lot of time these days doing church work ("I'm one of Jehovah's Witnesses") and is a devotee of true-crime programs on TV, marveling at the tactics and techniques of modern law enforcement. She couldn't fathom why the Jackson police hadn't solved her nephew's murder. The only answer, it seemed to her, was that the department didn't care enough to really try—a suspicion, for Southern black folks, that is not without historical foundation.

There had been a strong fraternal display at Bond's funeral. He had worked as a cop in Memphis and Murfreesboro before becoming chief in Bradford and then a deputy sheriff. He had served in the US Navy and then as a captain in the Army National Guard, deploying frequently, and had done tours in both Afghanistan and Iraq. At forty-one, he had more than twenty years of service in various uniforms. The long line of official mourners stretched around the block, representing all his old units and others from throughout western Tennessee. Some police came from as far as Nashville to pay respects—but from Jackson, his hometown, the force Bond had most wanted to join, no one showed. The family noticed.

And they thought they knew why. Over Bond's head was a cloud he could not shake. He was known to have "ties" with known criminals, gang members, and drug dealers—it was why, despite his repeated applications, the Jackson police had declined to hire him. Spanky's thrived partly by staying open so late, and it attracted some unsavory characters. Bond employed convicted felons. Some of his customers were gang-affiliated, and reports of gunfire at the location were common. The bar was considered by local cops to be a nuisance, an irritant to the public peace. And don't think they hadn't noticed Euhommie and Angela's nice home and the expensive cars in its driveway. Weighing their own earnings, they found the math wanting. Bond getting killed in gunplay at three a.m. outside Spanky's put him at a far cry from their definition of the "line of duty."

But to those who loved him, there was another way of seeing it. The Bonds were ambitious and exceptionally industrious. They were an attractive couple—Angela had the lean look of an athlete, although she was not inclined to work out like her husband, and wore her long black hair swept to one side and straight down to her shoulders. They glowed with health and were seemingly indefatigable. Angela owned and operated a beauty salon during the day and ran the busy bar and grill at night—most days she didn't head home until four in the morning. Euhommie's old Bradford police chief salary had been doubled by a grant from the NAACP because he'd been the first African American police chief in the town's history. And the job in the sheriff's office had been a step up. The impressive house and the cars also reflected Angela's willingness to borrow.

"I was guilty of having a lot of debt," she told me. "That was my problem, and, yeah, it was stupid. That's how we bought a lot of stuff."

And yes, Euhommie did have ties with known criminals, but so did everyone else in his large extended family—several members of which had themselves been in and out of jail. In his family and community, Euhommie was the exception. He employed a number of relatives with felony convictions at Spanky's, including his uncles Wilbur Bond, Arthur Hunt, and Charlie Reeves, and also old family friends like Eric Cobb. Perhaps partly *because* he had chosen policework and the military, he seemed intent on preserving those ties, keeping close to those who, as Sanders put it, "had chosen a different path."

"He had this soft spot, like, 'I can help them,'" she says. "'I can point them in the right direction.' He was always trying to give people feedback about 'the street life that you're living.' As opposed to me—if I help you once, then you're on your own— he always thought people deserved a second, third, fourth, fifth, and sixth chance, thinking, 'Eventually he's gonna get it right.' His thing was, 'If I can't help him, then who can?'"

A more tangible reason for the department's failure was the critical mistakes made in the beginning because the case had seemed so simple. A 9 mm round was recovered from Bond's body. Two 9 mm shell casings were found on the pavement near where he had fallen, and another spent 9 mm round was found near the building's front wall. One of the big front windows had been shattered, and a bullet had torn a hole in the metal frame of the bar's front door. Clearly, a shooter between Bond and the street had blazed from close range. Witnesses named two shooters, Michael Robinson and Steve "Black" Thomas, two young men with criminal pasts and gang connections. Accounts differed slightly—some had heard two pops, some three, some five—but three witnesses placed the blame for the killing shot squarely on Robinson.

Charlie Reeves, Bond's uncle, who was working security, said that his nephew had been fighting with both men. "Michael Robinson shot Euhommie," he told police, emphatically. "I saw his white shirt and dark gun. Black told me I was next." Reeves said that Bond had named Robinson as his shooter as he lay bleeding. Reeves added that "Black" Thomas had threatened him, saying, "We should have got both of y'all." Most of his story was backed by another uncle, Wilbert Bond.

Arthur Hunt, a third uncle, who was also working security in the parking lot outside, said he saw his nephew and Robinson fighting and had placed himself between the two. Some in the crowd tried to pull Robinson back, but he broke free, and Bond stepped from behind Hunt to confront him. Then came three gunshots, Hunt said, "from behind Mike." None hit Bond, who was still standing when Hunt heard a fourth shot, and his nephew fell. He said he saw both Robinson and Thomas running away, and that Robinson had a gun. He said the two left together in Thomas's car.

Another witness, Natalie Allen, said she was sitting in a car in the parking lot when the fight spilled outside. She saw Thomas run to his car, pop the hood, remove a handgun from underneath, and walk into the crowd around the fight, where she lost sight of him. She heard several gunshots and then saw Thomas run back with several others to his car and leave.

The Bond family was convinced, before the preliminary arraignment, outside the courthouse Angela was speaking angrily to her father about Lala Long, Robinson's mother.

"She knows her son did it!" she said.

"You don't have the right to say that because you didn't see anything," said Long, who had been standing behind her.

"You just keep on moving," Angela snapped at her. "Right now I've lost everything. You haven't lost anything."

The situation seemed clear enough. Within hours after Bond's death, Jackson police arrested Robinson and charged him with murder. Days later they arrested Thomas, charging him with aggravated assault and being an accessory to murder. The story got a lot of play in the local press, and the police department appeared to have handled the case efficiently. The department's chief told reporters confidently that the case, handled by one of its up-and-coming detectives, Tyreece Miller, had been wrapped up.

But when the witnesses were grilled by defense lawyers at a preliminary hearing a few days later, with the other witnesses out of the courtroom, their stories collapsed into a jumble of contradictions.

Reeves, who said he had been standing so close to his nephew that one of the rounds fired had passed through his own jacket, told the lawyers that he had seen Robinson fire the killing shot. He insisted he had seen Robinson and Thomas fleeing together, both armed, and that his dying nephew had fingered Robinson as the shooter.

Wilbur Bond, who had also named Robinson as the killer, now admitted that he had never stepped outside the bar.

Natalie Allen repeated her story: she'd seen Thomas pop the hood of his car, remove a gun, and then melt into the crowd before the gunshots began. But Allen said that Robinson was not one of the two men who had fled with Thomas. On cross-examination she also revealed that she was currently Robinson's girlfriend, something she had not told the police. The revelation threw suspicion on her account, which, by omitting her relationship to Robinson, might have been an attempt to exonerate him.

Arthur Hunt sat through a recitation of his criminal past before answering detailed questions about the night of the shooting. He now said that the first three shots he heard had come from behind him, not, as he had told police, from behind Robinson. He said Reeves had not been close to Bond, and that Robinson had been wearing a coat with a fur-lined hood, not the white T-shirt Reeves had described. He said that he saw Thomas fire, only to contradict himself seconds later, saying he'd seen Thomas pointing a gun but had not seen him shoot it. Hunt said he had stayed close to Bond as he lay on the pavement and that Bond, contrary to Reeves's testimony, did not name his killer.

"You sure about that?" asked Robinson's attorney, Joe Byrd.

"I'm positive. He didn't say anything."

Defense lawyers then called their own eyewitnesses, three of whom testified that Thomas alone had been fighting with Bond, and that Robinson had been inside the bar when the gunfire started. Erica Woods, Robinson's second cousin, described hiding behind a table with him when a man—who fit Angela Bond's description of their security guard Eric Cobb—ran in waving a gun and shouting, "Where's that nigger at! Y'all know what nigger I'm talking about!" She confirmed that Thomas left with two other men, neither of them Robinson, and that Thomas had been the one wearing a white T-shirt. Others then took the stand to corroborate these accounts. Robinson, they said, had not fled with Thomas; he had left in a separate vehicle driven by Wesley Cox, which Cox confirmed.

Then Robinson testified. He acknowledged previous criminal convictions—"I done served my time and ain't been in no trouble"—and gave his own version of events. He had come in with his cousin and friends. He had fought with neither Thomas nor Bond. He had not been armed. He was inside when the shooting occurred.

"Did you kill Mr. Bond?" his attorney asked.

"No, sir."

Judge Blake Anderson did not even wait for the defense to sum up. He referred the charges against Thomas to the grand jury, and dismissed all charges against Robinson. Angela ran from the courtroom crying.

Detective Miller, who had put the case together, slipped out before the hearing concluded, leaving his younger associate, Chris Chestnut, who was working his first homicide, to face the Bond family. The blame for Bond's death devolved into a family feud, the Bonds versus the Robinsons.

And then the case languished. Thomas, insisting that he had spent that entire evening at home with his girlfriend, was sent to jail after police found a weapon and drugs when they raided his apartment. But the weapon seized was not a 9 mm, and the witness accounts were too confused to support a charge. The strongest testimony against Thomas was from Robinson's girlfriend, Natalie Allen, and even she had not seen him shoot. One witness had testified that he saw Thomas shooting in Bond's direction from a distance, but this meant he could not have fired the killing shot. There had been stippling on Bond's body, powder-burn marks left a by weapon fired at close range.

* * *

Tyreece Miller, who would eventually be promoted to deputy commissioner, dropped the question into Chestnut's lap. The younger detective tried reinterviewing the witnesses, an exercise that got him nowhere. Perhaps fearing that they would be charged with perjury, since all of them could not have been telling the truth, most were uncooperative. Reeves ran whenever Chestnut approached him. The detective had Thomas transported back for further questioning, but the man just sat across the table and smirked at him. He knew he hadn't killed Bond and that there was no evidence he had. He had no incentive to say a thing. The thick case file sat on a shelf over Chestnut's desk like a bruise, a black mark on his career and on the entire department, but he could not see how to advance it.

An unsolved murder festers. The entire Bond clan was fed up with the Jackson police; just as they had spurned him in life, they were disrespecting him in death. It also sent an ugly message to the African American community. If the police wouldn't aggressively investigate the murder of a fellow officer, what did that say about their efforts for other black victims?

Angela sold her businesses, collected her husband's insurance and death benefits, and moved with their two sons to Atlanta.

"My husband took care of us in his life," she says, "and he took care of us in his death."

But that very windfall threw suspicion her way. There was plenty of motive, it was said, even beyond insurance money, pensions, and death benefits. Euhommie, after all, had not worked hard to hide his relationships with other women. Some believed he might have been killed by an angry husband or boyfriend.

"All the ugly stuff they're saying, that I had him killed or that another guy killed my husband 'cause he was dating his baby mama, you know, it was just so hurtful for me," Angela says. "Don't get me wrong, I'm not saying my husband was innocent, but at the end of the day . . . he took time and he took care of his family. And we saw eye to eye, and we were a team. He didn't do anything so disrespectful to me to the point where he brought women to the house. And so there's a lot of people looking at me and saying I'm stupid for not believing that that's why he got killed. You know, talk among yourselves, because I'm still Mrs. Bond, I still have his kids, and that's still the love of my life. So at the end of the day, that doesn't move me. And you're going to hear all that stuff too, and we were going through a divorce. I haven't signed any papers, show me some papers I've signed. I never did, and I had no plans to do it."

Debra Perry's thoughts wandered down that path. She believed the couple was going to divorce and that Angela was not happy about it—and the payout after her nephew's death had been considerable. She didn't feel good about these suspicions, but she had always seen Angela as grasping.

"I think she's a gold digger," Perry had told Euhommie after he'd first introduced Angela to her.

"But I don't have anything, Auntie," he'd said.

"I know, but she'll find a way to make money off of you."

And, as Perry saw it, she had.

It was in the midst of all this ugliness growing from the mystery of who shot Bond that Perry, watching one of her true-crime shows, saw Ken Brennan. A retired DEA agent and former Long Island cop, Brennan was a celebrated private investigator. On the program Perry watched, he had cleverly solved a mystery that had long stumped police in Florida. A muscular man with a shock of white hair, a gold chain around his thick neck, and rings on his fingers, Brennan looked the part of the hard-bitten detective. Sunglasses, leather jacket, motorcycle, and cigar enhanced his gruff, plainspoken style. "This is who I am supposed to use," thought Perry. She found Brennan's website online. Sanders made contact by e-mail and sent Brennan some information about Bond's case. Then Perry called him and began to grill him about his background and experience.

"Look, lady," he growled, "you reached out to me; I didn't reach out to you."

He said he would get back to her. The two women thought they'd never hear from him again. He called to say he'd take the case.

Brennan was expensive. Just to retain his services cost Perry and Sanders as much as they had spent for the reward and the posters. Perry had a comfortable nest egg; she had been the sole beneficiary when her husband, a veteran, died suddenly of a heart attack, and she had then sold their house. Sanders had a good state job. They sought help from the rest of the family, without success. One relative told Perry that Euhommie had once said that if anything ever happened to him, he didn't want it investigated.

"That didn't make sense," she told me. "I'm telling you right now, if you ever hear anybody say that Debra Bond Perry said, 'Don't ever investigate if I come up missing,' that's not true."

Another family member said she had already paid a private detective $24,000 and had learned nothing. Sanders asked for his name. They would contact him and pass along whatever he had learned to Brennan. "I don't remember his name," she was told. Perry scoffed. She told me, "Let me give you twenty-four thousand dollars and see if I ever forget *your* name."

She and her niece put up the money. Perry saw Brennan's acceptance of the case as nothing less than miraculous—as she put it, "A sign from God's Holy Spirit."

Brennan gets a lot of requests. Articles and TV reports of his successes, like the one seen by Perry, ensure a steady stream of random calls and referrals from law enforcement. Of necessity, he turns most away, either because they fail to sufficiently pique his interest or because he concludes, after a preliminary review, that he wouldn't be able to help. Those he doesn't take he refers to others—"I try to never leave a family hanging," he says.

As he saw it, the Bond case, seven years old, was as cold as cold could be. One thing grabbed him about it, though. When he called Perry to take the case, he told her, "I can't believe this guy was a police officer, and he was shot *seven years ago*, and nobody had been arrested for it."

It bugged him. As he saw it, "Some asshole has been walking around the state of Tennessee for the last seven years bragging that he had shot a cop and got away with it." That alone was enough to make him take the case. When he heard that Bond had served in both Iraq and Afghanistan—"This fucking guy served his country and his community," he said—he was sold.

Brennan visited Jackson for the first time in April 2015. It is a nondescript city of about sixty-five thousand, roughly halfway between Memphis and Nashville, an old railroad junction and onetime cotton hub. Today it is home to a few big factories, two of the largest being an aluminum mill that is a subsidiary of Toyota and a Kellogg's plant that produces Pringles. With lots of open ground, it feels more like a town than a city. It is mostly working class, split fairly even racially between whites and blacks. A significant portion of its population—15 percent—is considered poor. Much of Jackson is residential—neighborhoods of small one-story houses with tiny yards. Its main avenues, like Hollywood Drive, where Spanky's was located, are lined with strip malls. North of the city, near Interstate 40, the east–west highway that connects Memphis and Nashville, are a Walmart, newer shopping centers, movie theaters, chain restaurants and hotels, and Union University, an evangelical Christian school.

Brennan's first stop was to see Chris Chestnut, by then a sergeant in the department's criminal investigation unit, and two of his colleagues, Lieutenant Phil Stanfill and a newcomer, Detective Nick Donald. For Brennan, their cooperation was crucial. When Debra Perry bad-mouthed the department to him, he stopped her. "Look, the police are our friends in this," he said. "I can't do anything here without their help." His goal, he assured the detectives, was to help them, not to show them up.

Chestnut, Stanfill, and Donald were at first a little starstruck and disbelieving. Brennan seemed over the top. He looked to Donald as if he had walked in off a Hollywood set, a little larger than life, with the tan, the muscles, the jewelry, the sunglasses. But his blunt, profane way of putting things appealed to them. He talked like a cop. Brennan took Chestnut to lunch and explained his method, his affection and respect for all cops, and his need for their help. He said he had "no fucking interest" in what had happened earlier with the case, in finding fault or assigning blame. He said, "I'm looking strictly forward on this."

Policework had been Chestnut's entire schooling; he'd joined the department right out of high school, working as an emergency dispatcher before doing patrol work and graduating to detective. He too looked the part, with his shaved head and sunglasses, muscled arms sleeved with colorful tattoos, and a shield and handgun clipped to the belt of his jeans. Ken Brennan struck him as cocky, in a good way. "It's OK to be arrogant," says Chestnut, "if you've got something to be arrogant about." The private investigators (PIs) he'd encountered previously tended to be lazy, slippery, and ill-informed, more scammers than anything. They'd show up, glean what they could from the police, and then charge their clients for what they might have learned if they'd asked the cops themselves. Brennan was getting paid, but Chestnut could tell that he wasn't in it just for the money. The Bond case was the worst thing that had happened on Chestnut's watch. The case file haunted him daily. He had not only failed to solve it, he had been part of an effort to hang it on the wrong man.

Over lunch and then back at the department's offices, a characterless bunker of a building in downtown Jackson with mud-brown cinder-block walls, Chestnut shared the file with Brennan—crime-scene photos, hand-drawn maps, physical evidence, and piles of witness statements. There were pictures of Bond, newly deceased, stretched out prone on the operating table, eyes open, clothing torn away, a powerful man who clearly shouldn't have been dead. Other than a small cut over his right eye and single clean bullet wound in his upper right abdomen, he looked sturdy enough to compete in a decathlon. The killing round had left a small hole; it had a downward trajectory and had not exited, coming to rest in his iliac vein. He had bled out internally.

Chestnut presented his overview. A fight had broken out in the bar, and Bond had pushed it outside, where he'd tussled with either Robinson or Thomas—accounts varied. Shots were fired. One 9 mm round hit Bond; another ricocheted off the metal frame of the front door and was found on the pavement nearby. The big window to the right of the door was shattered. Three 9 mm shell casings were recovered on the pavement. He explained how witnesses had first named Robinson, but their accounts had not held up. Chestnut described his frustration in trying to reinterview them.

Brennan listened politely, taking it all in, admiring the stacks of reports, absorbing Chestnut's understanding of the event. Then he told him to forget all of it.

"Let's go take a look," he said.

Brennan likes physical evidence. Witnesses are often more trouble than they are worth; as he puts it, "they're a fuckin' pain in the ass." Memory is imprecise, even when people are trying to help. Witnesses claim to have seen things they did not see, and deny seeing things they did. Sometimes they are afraid to say what they did see, and sometimes they are too eager to describe things they did not. They exaggerate; they lie; they shade the truth; they even take advantage of situations to settle old scores. What doesn't change, what is not subject to distortion or dissembling or forgetfulness, are the facts. So, as he explained to Chestnut and Stanfill, the *right way* to start is to empty your head of everything anyone has told you. Find out for yourself. Let the facts speak. The facts give you solid ground, the only point of reference you can trust. Only then do you start questioning witnesses, matching memories against what you can know for sure.

The building that had housed Spanky's Bar & Grill was at the southeast end of a sad, nondescript strip mall inaptly named Hollywood Plaza. What Brennan saw was a line of unadorned storefronts—a beauty salon, a vacuum cleaner store,

a consignment clothing shop. On the faded brown vertical sid-
ing above, there were dark patches where signs for now-defunct
businesses had once hung. Across the street is a lumberyard. The
old Spanky's building, now home to a catering service, looked
the same as it did in the old crime-scene photos. Fronting it was
a battered parking lot.

Chestnut set the scene. Bond had fallen in an empty parking
space just outside the front door. Beside him had been a parked
car. The detective noted where each of the 9 mm shell casings
had been found, one close to the front door, the other downhill
from Bond's feet. The metal frame on the left side of the front
door still had the hole made by the round they'd found on the
pavement a few feet away.

Brennan paced around and around, trying to picture the
scene. Across the lot, about fifty feet away, the crime-scene photographer had snapped pictures of spent .40 caliber shells, some
of them bent and scuffed. They had been duly collected but
not considered important. It was not uncommon for Spanky's
customers to discharge their weapons, often at the sky—the
department often responded to reports of such shooting—and
given the appearance of the shells, it was assumed they were old.
Bond had, after all, been hit by a 9 mm round.

Brennan believes everything the police note at a crime scene
is important. The trampled shells had made at least one cop on
the scene curious enough to photograph and bag them. That
was enough.

These .40 caliber shell casings had all been found within a
dozen feet of each other, about fifty feet from the victim. Brennan stood at that spot and looked across the lot at the building.
An unskilled right-handed shooter would find that the kick,

unless actively corrected, would pull his aim to the right. They had found a round that hit the door frame. To its right was the shattered window. Beyond that was just a patch of woods where other spent rounds would likely have landed—they had not been found.

Brennan walked around the lot and around the building and over to the patch of woods, thinking. Chestnut and Stanfill watched him curiously.

"Something ain't sitting right with me here," he told them. He said he wanted to go back and read through the reports.

Later that day, reviewing the files, Brennan came across Natalie Allen's statement. She had seen Thomas retrieve a gun from under the hood of his car and then run to a spot in the crowd near where the .40 shells were found. It confirmed Brennan's hunch.

Chestnut pointed out that Allen had been Robinson's girlfriend, and that her story had been considered nothing more than an effort to shift the blame from him to Thomas, but Brennan disagreed.

"She says here that he got the gun from under the car hood," he explained. "I think she's telling the truth. She's very specific about where the gun came from. She doesn't say that he gets a gun from underneath his car or from the back seat or the trunk, she says he pops the hood. Somebody who has been arrested, he knows that if cops pull him over they might toss his car, but they're not going to bother pulling the fucking hood up and taking a look under there. That's something a gang member would do. She ain't making that up."

They went back out to the crime scene a day later, pulling out all the stops to oblige Brennan. Chestnut got the fire department to bring out a ladder truck so they could search surrounding rooftops for spent rounds. They used a laser pointer to confirm the shooting angles from where the .40 caliber shell casings had been found to the damage on the building's front. The day was sweltering, and it took hours, and in the end, while they didn't find any other rounds, Brennan was certain.

"I think there was a shootout here," he said, standing where the .40 caliber shells had been found. "I think there were two guys shooting. Chris, you know that round you recovered that hit the door frame? Do you still have it?"

They did.

"What caliber is it?"

"Nine millimeter."

"Listen, do you mind going back there with me? Let's just check. Maybe I'm wrong, but I don't think that it's a nine millimeter; I think it's a forty. I know the property clerk is going to be pissed off, digging this shit up from seven years ago. It's a pain in the ass, but let's just do it. Humor me."

It was a .40 caliber round.

When Chestnut had inherited the case from Miller, he'd been told that the round recovered from the pavement in front of the bar was 9 mm. He had never checked for himself. When he looked back at the file, he saw that even the old evidence sheet had noted that the round had been .40 caliber. He hadn't checked it. He felt foolish and said so.

"It wasn't even your fucking case to begin with," Brennan reassured him. "But one thing I learned a long time ago: Don't rely on what some cop told you somebody said, or what somebody says they did. Find out for yourself. Then you know it's done, because you did it."

So the scene was not as it had been envisioned. Bond had not simply been shot at close range by a single gunman. There had been two shooters: one near the victim, the other across the lot. Since there was no evidence of another 9 mm round in or around the building, even though one had been fired several times, it led Brennan to suspect that whoever was firing that gun had been primarily aiming, not at Bond, but at someone else. The two gunmen had been shooting at each other.

Brennan made six trips to Jackson over the next year and a half. Most of his time there was spent in the company of either Chestnut, Stanfill, or Donald. He tracked down dozens of witnesses and sought out Bond's relatives and friends, including cops who had served alongside him. He met Angela Bond at the airport in Atlanta, where they had a long conversation. She replayed for him her memory of that chaotic, tragic morning.

He developed a deeper feel for the victim. He got that Bond had been a ladies' man and that he loved attention, and he heard the suspicions about his ties with criminals and drug dealers, but his own impression of the man ran deeper. Bond had clearly loved being a cop, and his race and upbringing made him a uniquely valuable one, even if his hometown force hadn't recognized it. He was able to bridge the wall of hostility and suspicion between cops and community. Bond had disliked wearing his gun, often leaving it in his patrol car, where it was found the night of his death. He could hold his own physically with anyone, and he did not hesitate to show this off. Once, while reporting a robbery in progress, he said the suspect was fleeing on foot. "Give me thirty seconds," he said. Sure enough, thirty seconds later, winded, he returned with the suspect in cuffs. He

believed, as his sister said, in giving people the benefit of the
doubt. He was a peacemaker. His instinct was not to confront
people but to calm them, to reason with them. It was the role he
played at Spanky's when things got out of hand. Brennan could
picture him jumping over the bar to break up a fight, absorbing
some punishment yet shouting for everyone to calm down, and
then steering the troublemaker out the door.

Only in this case, tragically, the confrontation had not been
defused.

Brennan didn't just interview witnesses, he brought them
back to the parking lot of Hollywood Plaza to walk him through
their memory of the night. This would prove, to Chestnut, the
most useful of his tactics, because being at the crime scene not
only helped them remember more clearly, it corrected what they
misremembered. They could see, for instance, that only certain
things could have been seen or heard from where they had been
standing. It also allowed Brennan to more confidently fit their
stories to the physical evidence.

It helped that Brennan was not a cop, but it also helped
that he approached everyone calmly and respectfully. He was
fact-finding, not cross-examining. If someone's story didn't
make sense, he didn't accuse them of lying or lean on them or
threaten; instead, he showed them how they had to be wrong.

The best example was Charlie Reeves, who had testified with
such certainty against Michael Robinson. He'd done his best
since to avoid Chestnut. So when Brennan and the detective went
to Reeves's house, they stayed in the back seat of Brennan's rented
black Cadillac and sent the PI's assistant, a woman, to the door.

A jittery, hyper-expressive man with a history of cocaine
troubles, Reeves didn't answer the door. When Brennan's

assistant walked back out to the Caddy and leaned in to talk to him and Chestnut, Reeves stepped out, eyeing them nervously. Chestnut felt certain he was about to bolt, especially when he and Brennan stepped out of the car. Reeves was subject to court-ordered regular urine tests, and to the sergeant it looked like he had reason to worry. But in the struggle between flight and curiosity, curiosity prevailed.

"Holy shit, man, they told me my uncle won the lottery!" he explained when Brennan and Chestnut approached. "I seen a brand-new Cadillac and a white lady at my door, so I figure it must be my uncle. That's the only reason I answered the door."

Once he started talking, he couldn't stop. Right there in the yard, he threw himself into a dramatic reenactment of the night Bond was shot, moving around his yard, crouching, throwing imaginary punches. At one point he dropped to the ground and kicked up his legs. Chestnut noticed an old woman walking nearby, carrying grocery bags. She slowed and stared. The detective could only wonder what she thought. Here was her neighbor, throwing a seeming fit, surrounded by two white men and a white woman. Chestnut waved to her, and she walked on hastily without looking back.

Reeves had said all along that he had been standing right next to Bond when he was shot, so close that one of the bullets had passed right through his jacket. He had holes in his jacket to prove it. But when they took him to the parking lot, Brennan contradicted him.

"There's no way you could have been right next to Euhommie," he said. He showed him a photo from the crime scene, indicating where Reeves had dropped his sunglasses and bandana, asking, "Whose shit was this?"

"That was mine!"

The objects were up next to the front wall of the bar, about ten feet or more from the victim. Brennan knew that one of the .40 caliber rounds, likely fired by Thomas, had ricocheted off the front door frame and shattered the window alongside it before coming to rest on the pavement nearby. Given where Reeves's things had been found against the wall, it made sense that this was the round that had passed through his jacket.

"We know you had to be by the fuckin' window," Brennan said.

Reeves admitted that this made sense and altered his recollection. He now said that the only person close to his nephew had been Eric Cobb.

Brennan tried to talk to Steve Thomas, who in the ensuing years had been released from prison. After arranging to meet the investigators at his place, Thomas wasn't there when they showed up. Thomas's brother phoned him and put him on speakerphone.

"You were supposed to meet us here," said Donald.

Thomas made an excuse.

"What are you, a pussy?" erupted Brennan. "Get your ass over here like you promised and look me in the fuckin' eye like a man."

There was silence on Thomas's end, and then he complained to Donald, "Why is he talking to me like that?"

"I'm from New York," said Brennan. "I talk like that to everybody."

Thomas stayed away.

Brennan traveled with Donald to interview another witness, Daniel Cole, who was serving a prison term. They encountered a sour, unhelpful man. Cole told them that his father had been murdered when he was a child, and the police had done nothing about it. He said, "Why the fuck should I help you?" He then refused to answer Brennan's questions. When Cole did speak, it was to offer a snide comment about the other witnesses Brennan mentioned.

As the two detectives drove away from the prison, Donald remarked, "That was a complete waste of time."

"No, it wasn't," said Brennan.

"He didn't tell us a thing!"

"Yes, he did."

"What?"

"Remember when I brought up Eric Cobb and said that some people remembered that he had a gun that night? Cole said, 'If fuckin' Cobb had a gun, he was shooting it.' Meaning, Cobb is a trigger-happy son of a bitch."

Angela Bond had told of Cobb on a table in the bar, waving a handgun, shouting "Where's the motherfucker at?" or words to that effect. Others had also remembered this. If Cobb had been the only one standing close to Bond, could he have fired the mortal round?

Cobb didn't know he had become Brennan's prime suspect when he was asked to pay a visit back to the crime scene. A stocky, middle-aged man, he had been a friend of the Bond family for years. Euhommie had overlooked his felony conviction to employ him as a security guard. Cobb appeared wary about answering questions, but he agreed to come along. As he paced through his movements that night, he confirmed the account he had given to police right after the shooting, placing himself just two feet from Bond when he fell. But he insisted that he had been unarmed. As a convicted felon, he was not allowed to possess a handgun.

"What are you talkin' about?" said Brennan. "There's people who saw a gun in your hand!"

Cobb had an explanation. He did have a gun that night, he said, but only later, after Bond had been shot. He said he had called his wife to tell her there was shooting at the bar, and that she had driven over immediately to bring him the gun.

Brennan left Cobb with the other detectives, walked across the parking lot, and phoned Cobb's wife. When she rolled up a few minutes later, he hustled out to the car to greet her first and asked if she had brought her husband a gun that night.

She said she had not.

On the evening of Tuesday, July 18, 2016, on his last visit to Jackson, Brennan delivered his answer to his clients, Perry and Sanders, and other Bond family members in a conference room at the city's DoubleTree Hotel. Chestnut, Stanfill, and Donald were there, as was Jody Pickens, the area's district attorney. Angela Bond couldn't make the trip from Atlanta. Cobb was invited, and while he initially said he planned to attend, he didn't show up. Perhaps he saw where things were headed.

Brennan pieces together his findings painstakingly. He does his best thinking early in the morning when he can't sleep. He ruminates about his cases, trying to complete the puzzles. He's not happy unless everything fits, and then, when it does, he's certain. His process is about more than physical evidence and memory; it involves everything he has learned about the people involved and what he knows about people

in general. It had led him to understand how Eric Cobb had
killed his good friend.

There was a great deal of tension in the room. The family
arrived with its long-standing resentment of the police. Pickens
didn't improve the mood by reminding everyone at the outset
that seven years had elapsed, and that no matter what Brennan
had found, his office would be bound by Tennessee's statutes of
limitations. This kicked off an exchange of grievances. Brennan
lost his patience.

"Hey, listen," he shouted. "One thing I need all of you to
do is be quiet and listen to what I have to say. I don't want to be
interrupted. Not once. I'm going to give you a presentation, and
I'm going to tell you what happened to Euhommie. And after
the end of it, you're going to know exactly what happened. And
then, when I'm done, you can ask me anything that you want."

The room quieted.

Brennan then walked them through the scene step-by-
step, digressing to point out how he had reached each of his
conclusions. There was a fight inside the bar, which Bond had
steered outside. Steve Thomas went to his car and retrieved a
gun from under the hood—Brennan explained why he found
this testimony believable. The .40 caliber shells found in a
group on the lot about fifty feet away showed that shots had
been fired from there, and a .40 caliber handgun was found at
that site. The damaged front of the bar showed that a round
had hit from that direction, and the round recovered from the
front was consistent with that gun. The laser had shown how
the angles of those shots lined up. Cobb had then stepped
out the front door, to see Thomas either approaching with a

gun or shooting. Despite his denial, Brennan was convinced that Cobb had a gun with him, a 9 mm. Standing near the building, he shot at Thomas, either returning fire or initiating it. Bond, the peacemaker, then tried to stop the shooting. Everything Brennan had learned about the victim suggested this is what the victim would have done. He reached for his friend's gun—Reeves had said he heard his nephew say, "Give me the gun," just before he was shot—and it went off. This explained the stippling around the death wound—Brennan had double-checked with the medical examiner to confirm the exact nature of the powder and burns.

"The gun would have to have been fired from no more than two feet away," Brennan said.

This also explained the trajectory of the killing round. It had traveled downward through Bond's torso. If Robinson or Thomas or anyone else had fired the shot from farther away, the trajectory of the bullet would have been upward, and there would have been no stippling. It also explained why one of the 9 mm shells was found below Bond's feet where he lay on the pavement. It had been fired where Euhommie had been standing and then rolled downhill—the pavement sloped gently down. It was not clear that Cobb even realized in those moments that he had shot his friend. He had, according to Angela, run into the bar looking for the shooter. But Brennan was sure that Cobb eventually knew. He had questioned him in detail, and his evasive answers were revealing. He was not surprised that Cobb had not shown up.

"It's the only way it could have happened," Brennan concluded. The room was silent. "OK," he said, "Do you have any questions?"

No one did. They all just looked at him. His explanation fit the facts and made sense. All of them had known both Euhommie and Eric.

"I just want to know why that motherfucker never said anything!" one of Euhommie's uncles complained.

"Hey, listen," Brennan said. "Be that as it may, this ultimately ends up being an accident. He thought he was doing his job. He was there for security, and he was trying to protect the club and protect Euhommie."

Pickens interrupted.

"That's a good theory," he said, "but it's just a theory."

"Hey, listen," said Brennan, addressing the family. "I understand where the district attorney is coming from, but this ain't no theory. This is *exactly* what happened."

And then something occurred that floored Chestnut. One by one, the family members present said that they had known it all along. Someone had heard that Cobb had told someone else that he knew who shot Euhommie. Another had heard that Eric had admitted it years earlier. There was agreement all around. Brennan had confirmed what they now said they had known all along.

"I was so taken aback," said the detective. "Jody Pickens, he about fell out of his chair. Like, 'Wait a minute, you've known about this the whole time?'"

They hadn't. The story about Cobb's "confession" had been nothing more than a rumor until Brennan's careful reconstruction. He had congealed it into a certainty. If they had all known, why would Perry, Sanders, and Angela Bond have put up a $15,000 reward for tips and paid for posters on city buses? Why would Perry and Sanders have hired Brennan?

"I told Ken at the beginning, I didn't know what happened," Perry told me. "He took our case, and he didn't have to. He took a little hick town, Jackson, Tennessee, and came to check on us little people down here." When Brennan finished, her opinion of the police, of Chris Chestnut in particular, and of Pickens had improved, and they were more attentive to her. "They saw that I hadn't just been sitting on my thong," she says. "I got all these people involved. I felt totally relieved when Ken was finished with my case."

The truth rarely pleases everyone. Brennan tells all of his clients that whatever their motive in hiring him, and whatever outcome they desire, he will attempt only one thing, to tell them exactly what happened. The rest he cannot control.

No one in the Bond family or on the Jackson police force doubts that Brennan delivered in this case. Perry said she and Sanders feel Brennan did everything he promised he would. Angela told me that she had heard the rumor about Cobb but had never believed it. Knowing has not resolved all of the pain, bitterness, and division. Some in the family left the DoubleTree meeting disgruntled, especially after Pickens reiterated that it was too late to prosecute Cobb for either involuntary manslaughter, the most appropriate charge, or illegal gun possession. There was nothing his office could do.

Cobb has never admitted to the charge, despite heroic efforts to persuade him.

"I texted him, and he said he would meet me, and he didn't," says Perry. "We're not vengeful. I wouldn't do anything to him. But he won't meet with us because he knows that we know."

Perry regrets her early suspicions of Euhommie's wife, Angela. "It is not something I'm proud of," she says. They have patched things up, somewhat.

For her part, Angela regrets confronting Michael Robinson's mother at the preliminary hearing. "You know, probably naturally I'm going to say ugly things because that's my husband, but I probably shouldn't have said what I said." She remains angry at Brennan for, she says, refusing to lay the case out completely for her. She says he told her that she was not his client. Brennan says he did explain his finding to her.

Chris Chestnut, now a lieutenant, is simply amazed by what Brennan accomplished. He calls it "magic."

"It was an absolute pleasure working with him. I'll be honest with you; I wish I could afford to hire him on some other cold cases that I have right now, because I'm pretty confident that with his efforts and mine, I think we could get a lot of things solved." He and Phil Stanfill said they learned things working with Brennan that they now routinely apply to their own cases.

The Bond case will continue to stare down at Chestnut from his shelf until Cobb admits what happened. Chestnut recruited a prominent African American judge to reach out to Cobb in an effort to reassure him that there will be no criminal consequences for telling his story, to no avail.

The detective has his own suspicions about why the family never told him what they had heard about Cobb: "The only mention of Eric Cobb is he's on the other end of the parking lot working security and hears gunfire. None of the other witnesses put him anywhere around the shooting. I think it's because they knew. I think the whole reason they came up with the Michael

Robinson story was to protect Cobb. He's known the family for years."

One of the uncles, Wilbur Bond, who positively identified Robinson as the shooter, had reason to hold a grudge against him—Robinson had punched him in the face several years earlier and knocked out some of his teeth.

It is more likely that, with only a vague suspicion about Cobb, the family was reluctant to share the idea with police. He had been, after all, a friend.

There will be no legal reckoning for the shooting of Euhommie Bond. The cop, the veteran, the celebrated ladies' man, the brother, nephew, husband, and father, the determined peacemaker, trying to stop a gunfight outside his bar, was killed by a friend, victim of a violent world that he didn't have the heart to leave.